DATE DUE		JUN 28'99
APR 7 1992	JUN 6	FEB 1 6
JUL 2 7 1992	FEB 2 0 '97	
FEB 2 3 1993	MAR 1 5 '97	
MAR 2 1993	APR 3 '97	
MAR 1 7 1993	APR 11 '97	
APR 5 1993		
		MAR 2 3 '98
FEB 7 1994		NOV 2 3 '98
MAR 1 5 1995		JAN 6 '99

D1010935

A PERFECT BRIGHTNESS OF HOPE

A PERFECT BRIGHTNESS OF HOPE

ANITA R. CANFIELD

Deseret Book Company
Salt Lake City, Utah

Library of Congress Cataloging-in-Publication Data

Canfield, Anita, 1946–
    A perfect brightness of hope / Anita R. Canfield
        p. cm.
    ISBN 0-87579-481-5
    1. Hope—Religious aspects—Christianity. 2. Christian life—
Mormon authors. 3. Canfield, Anita, 1946–   . I. Title.
BV4638.C26   1991
234'.2—dc20   91-55239
                                                        CIP

Printed in the United States of America

10   9   8   7   6   5   4   3   2   1

Contents

Preface

Some parts of this volume came easily, and some "cost" quite a bit more. My desire in sharing these thoughts is to offer words of love, encouragement, hope, and perhaps to help you set in motion thoughts that can turn into actions that will cause positive changes in your life. My desire is to help.

That desire has been born from the overwhelming gratitude I feel for the spiritual gift of hope. That gift played a key part in the rescue of my son.

Please look past the imperfection you see in me and in my writing. The principles contained in these pages are true and perfect; the presenter is not. The credit for the good works and testimony you find within belongs to the Savior and to him alone. The goodness of Jesus Christ and his gospel bring the only true light and hope into our lives.

Chapter One

A Perfect Brightness of Hope

Some time ago I listened to an interview with the wife of a prominent politician about her battle against alcohol and drug abuse. At one point Barbara Walters asked her if she had felt like giving up completely, especially after her family discovered her problem. She answered, "No. There were times I saw a *glimmer* of hope." In the midst of despair and even desperation (she drank nail polish remover and rubbing alcohol after her family had removed all the liquor from their home), she was able to still see a glimmer of hope.

There is something so eternal, so God natured about each of us, that in times of deepest faithlessness we are still able to muster a glimmer of hope. That may be good enough for some, but it isn't good enough for candidates for the celestial kingdom. Nephi instructed us expertly as one who too had struggled for hope in his life:

"Wherefore, ye must press forward with a steadfastness in Christ, having a perfect brightness of hope, and a love of God and of all men. Wherefore, if ye shall press forward, feasting upon the word of Christ, and endure to the end, behold, thus saith the Father: Ye shall have eternal life" (2 Nephi 31:20).

How can we turn a "glimmer" into a "perfect brightness" of hope? Can we? Is hope only for a chosen few? Is hope really that important? Didn't we come here for a trial of our faith, not of our hope? Can we have a "perfect" brightness of hope when we struggle with so much imperfection? And what is it we shall hope for?

Hope, we are taught by Moroni, not only is a mighty spiritual gift that comes close on the heels of faith but also is absolutely necessary to building faith:

"And again, my beloved brethren, I would speak unto you concerning hope. *How is it that ye can attain unto faith, save ye shall have hope?* . . .

"Wherefore, if a man have faith he must needs have hope; for without faith there cannot be any hope" (Moroni 7:40, 42; italics added).

But there was once a day I couldn't understand what a weak idea like hope had to do with a strong idea like faith. As it does for most people, the word *hope* meant for me a weak and wishful thought. I used *hope* to mean an expression of a feeble wish overshadowed by a strong doubt:

"We hope it doesn't snow."

"I hope I won't get sick."

"I hope I marry a millionaire."

My increased understanding came after learning that the synonym for the word *hope* is *expect*. Hope is not a wish but an *expectation*. Look at the meaning of the following scriptures when we substitute *expect* for *hope:*

"And again, my beloved brethren, I would speak unto you concerning hope [expectation]. How is it that ye can attain unto faith, save ye shall have hope [expectation]?" (Moroni 7:40).

"Be of good courage, and he shall strengthen your heart, all ye that hope [expect] in the Lord" (Psalms 31:24).

"Wherefore, whoso believeth in God might with surety

hope [expect] for a better world, yea, even a place at the right hand of God, which hope [expectation] cometh of faith, maketh an anchor to the souls of men, which would make them sure and steadfast, always abounding in good works, being led to glorify God" (Ether 12:4).

Hope, then, is an expectation of things to come. We must *expect* to be raised up through faith and obedience to eternal life. We must *expect* we can become as Christ and inherit the celestial kingdom.

"And what is it that ye shall hope [expect] for? Behold I say unto you that ye shall have hope [expectation] through the atonement of Christ and the power of his resurrection, *to be raised unto life eternal,* and this because of your faith in him according to the promise" (Moroni 7:41; italics added).

Hope, then, is a principle of power. Some people think they have to fast and pray so that everything will be okay *now.* They do it, and then when everything doesn't turn out okay, they think they don't have enough faith or that God doesn't care. Everything is not always going to be okay *now.* Fasting and praying are to strengthen our faith and hope. Our faith and hope are what will carry us through the not-okay stuff.

When I was about twelve years old, I heard a sacrament meeting speaker who kept apologizing for his talk. He kept saying he didn't feel worthy to present the material. He felt others in the congregation were more qualified. He made it clear he wasn't sure he could gain the celestial kingdom.

As the years passed, I heard that same attitude expressed by members many times. I assumed the celestial kingdom wasn't for ordinary people like me. It would require perfection in this life. Only prophets, bishops, and Relief Society presidents could make it. Not until my late twenties did I realize that that kind of thinking has no place in the gospel of Jesus Christ. The gospel actually helps us to have hope. The Lord *wants* us to have hope. He even says it is a requirement for exaltation:

"For no man can be saved, according to the words of Christ, save they shall have faith in his name. . . . How is it that ye can attain unto faith, save ye shall have hope?" (Moroni 7:38–40).

If we don't hope—*expect*—to get to the celestial kingdom, then what are we doing in this church? We can get as much hope, or lack of it, from any other organization on the earth. This is the only gospel and church that require enough sacrifice to produce sufficient faith to develop a "perfect brightness of hope."

Hope and faith are not only interrelated but interdependent. With that understanding, then, let's change the phrase "have faith" to "do faith." Many instances in my life have taught me that faith is an action concept, not a passive concept. Perhaps no instance has had so profound an effect as one involving one of my own children.

Ashley struggled all her life for her grades. She was diligent and concerned and tried her best to succeed, but it was hard for her to retain concepts and do the work. Because of her poor grades and despite her diligent efforts, she was always discouraged.

We hired tutors. From the fourth grade on she was tutored extensively to help her grasp concepts and keep up with her work. It was painful for all of us. Then at the end of her freshman year of high school, she received final grades of Ds and Fs. For the first time the light went out of her eyes. It seemed as if there now was not even a glimmer of hope.

We have a yearly family tradition. On the night of the first day of school, we all receive a father's (in my case, husband's) blessing. He begins with the youngest child and asks each of us if there is anything special we need.

The first school night of Ashley's sophomore year, when

her turn came, she was asked the familiar and standard question, "Anything special, Ashley?" There was no reply. Suddenly the tears could no longer be contained. Quietly weeping she asked, "Dad, do you think Heavenly Father cares about my grades? I think he does. In my patriarchal blessing he says I have been given a keen mind and a mind that can retain what I learn. Dad, you know how hard I've tried! I've tried and tried. In my patriarchal blessing Heavenly Father says he wants me to go to college. How can I do that? Do you think there's a special blessing for me? I've tried—but, Dad, I'm dumb."

Steve put his arms around her and gently replied that he knew Heavenly Father cared about all parts of our lives. As her earthly father, didn't he care about her development? How much more would Heavenly Father care about her entire potential because only He knows just what's waiting for her?

He placed his hands on her head and blessed her with the usual admonitions to put aside extracurricular activities until schoolwork was done. He counseled to keep her priorities of church, family, school, and fun in the proper order. He blessed her with health, and safety, and then there was a long pause. I looked up and saw tears streaming down his cheeks. I knew that there was a special blessing and that indeed Heavenly Father cares. In essence, this is what came next:

"Ashley, a modern-day prophet has admonished us to read the Book of Mormon. He has even promised that those who make it part of their lives will have greater powers because of it. Ashley, Heavenly Father wants to enter into a covenant with you. If you will follow a prophet's voice and begin tonight to read the Book of Mormon every day—and not just read it, but study and ponder it; and not just this year, but begin tonight on a lifelong pursuit of reading and studying the scriptures every day—then he will bless you. He will bless you in your mind and in your ability and in your efforts. You will succeed, so much so that you will even be utterly amazed."

A tremendous spirit was present, and it bore witness to us of who the Author of that priesthood blessing was.

That night when I went to say good night, Ashley had the Book of Mormon open to 1 Nephi 1. She looked up and said, "Mom, will you answer a question?"

This is great, I thought. Already she wants more information!

"Mom, how can reading and studying the Book of Mormon help my grades?"

For a moment I was puzzled too, and then the answer became quite clear. "Ashley, I don't know. I don't know at all. But this much I do know: obedience is everything. Faith is a principal of obedience. If we obey, even though we don't understand, the Lord gives us power. For every law we obey, a blessing comes. Maybe we don't even know it at the time, but obeying brings blessings. Right now, Ashley, do you have the faith to obey, even though you don't understand?"

She said she did and absolutely wouldn't quit. She would "do faith."

And she did. She read the Book of Mormon faithfully. Not only did she not understand how it was all going to work but she didn't understand much of what she was reading.

The end of the first nine weeks came. She came into the kitchen after school, crying and clutching a crumpled piece of paper. She threw it on the counter and ran upstairs. I knew immediately it was the grade report, and my heart sank. How would I ever instill a desire for faith in her heart again? But as I uncrumpled the paper, there were all As and Bs! I ran upstairs and found her in the bathroom, splashing her face. Now we were both crying. Expecting a story of inspired new study procedures, I exclaimed "Ashley! How did you do it?"

Instead, my fifteen-year-old daughter taught me again about "doing faith" in three simple words, "Book of Mormon."

She just *did it.* She didn't understand why or how; she just obeyed. The Lord doesn't require us to be perfect, to understand, or even to agree with him. All he requires is "the heart and a willing mind" (D&C 64:34). If we are willing, we can be obedient. If we are obedient, we are immediately blessed with the gift of meekness. If we are meek, then we can receive the visitation of the Holy Ghost and all other spiritual gifts and powers we need to help us accomplish whatever task is before us.

At the end of the semester we received a letter from the high school congratulating us on Ashley's having made the honor roll. Enclosed was a bumper sticker that read "I am the proud parent of a Bonanza High Honor Roll student."

I posted this letter and bumper sticker on the door, and when she came home, we laughed and cheered and celebrated! When the clamor was over with she said, "Heavenly Father cares. He keeps his promises. Six months ago, who would have thought I'd be on the honor roll! All I wanted was better grades to get into college." Then she begged me to *please* not put that bumper sticker on the car.

At the end of the school year Ashley was on the honor roll again, and we received a letter telling us that she was being recommended for several distinguished scholar classes for the next school year. That summer she finished reading the Book of Mormon and began reading it again.

She continued to be on the honor roll throughout her remaining two years of high school. By the time she graduated, she had read the Book of Mormon three times and the Doctrine and Covenants once. Now she is in college, and she continues to read the scriptures daily.

Much, much more important than Ashley's "utterly amazing" success has been the sweet and pure testimony she has received of "doing faith" by obedience. Through faith and obedience she has truly gained a "perfect brightness of hope" in herself and in the Lord.

Obedience is everything. Once I questioned whether a person should be a free thinker or follow by blind faith. Now it seems to me the only important thing is obedience.

More than fifteen years ago I read an article that categorized Church members into iron rod members and liahona members. Basically the author said the iron rod members were those who followed by blind faith, like sheep following the shepherd's call. They never questioned anything, just did what they were told, and were often somewhat hard-line in their views. He implied that iron rods were often self-righteous. The liahonas were the opposite. They were free thinkers, philosophers, always questioning, inquisitive. They more often wanted confirmation before accepting doctrine or counsel. He implied that liahonas had a more liberal and sensitive approach to the gospel that allowed for greater individuality.

A few years ago a friend mentioned an article he thought I'd like to read. It was the same article I had read more than a decade before. My friend commented, "Anita, I thought you'd enjoy this. You'll also see that you are definitely an iron rod." Now, that startled me, because I distinctly remembered having decided when finishing it the first time that I was definitely a liahona!

I began to read the article again. I had read only the first few paragraphs when I knew something was very wrong. This material was not inspiring me, and it was hard to see truth present. Then clearly I realized that the issue is not whether we should be free thinkers or follow by blind faith; the issue is whether we will have willing hearts and minds and be obedient. If the article had been about being of one heart and one mind with Jesus Christ, the discussion would have been about submissiveness and obedience rather than about independence. Elder Spencer W. Kimball said:

"Is it blind obedience when the student pays his tuition, reads his text assignments, attends classes, and thus qualifies for his eventual degrees? . . .

"Is it blind obedience when one regards the sign 'High Voltage — Keep Away' or is it the obedience of faith in the judgment of experts who know the hazard?

"Is it blind obedience when the air traveler fastens his seat belt as that sign flashes or is it confidence in the experience and wisdom of those who know more of hazards and dangers?

"Is it blind obedience when the little child gleefully jumps from the table into the strong arms of its smiling father, or is this implicit trust in a loving parent who feels sure of his catch and who loves the child better than life itself?

"Is it blind obedience when an afflicted one takes vile-tasting medicine prescribed by his physician or yields his own precious body to the scalpel of the surgeon or is this the obedience of faith in one in whom confidence may safely be imposed?

"Is it blind obedience when the pilot guides his ship between the buoys which mark the reefs and thus keeps his vessel in deep water or is it confidence in the integrity of those who have set up protective devices?

"Is it then blind obedience when we, with our limited vision, elementary knowledge, selfish desires, ulterior motives, and carnal urges, accept and follow the guidance and obey the commands of our loving Father who begot us, created a world for us, loves us, and has planned a constructive program for us, wholly without ulterior motive, whose greatest joy and glory is to 'bring to pass the immortality and eternal life' of all his children?

"Blind obedience it might be when no agency exists, when

there is regimentation, but in all of the commands of the Lord given through his servants, there is total agency free of compulsion" (in Conference Report, Oct. 1954, p. 53).

Shortly after Steve and I were married, we decided to complete a year's supply of food storage. After about a year and a half of research, saving, buying, and planning, the day came when we put the last items into the designated closet. I stood back, looked at it, and said, "Steve, really, do you think someday we'll have to eat all this?"

He said, "It doesn't matter."

That made me get excited. "What do you mean it doesn't matter? We've just spent one and a half years and every extra penny we've had to get this together."

Quietly he reassured me with a truth that I've been learning ever since. He said, "It doesn't matter, that's all. A flood may come and wash this away. A fire may burn it all to ashes, or an earthquake could swallow it up. Or, we may have to walk away and leave it. Maybe we'll eat it; maybe not. It doesn't matter. This food isn't going to save us, Anita. *Obedience* is what will save us. We obeyed the prophet, we got this all together, and that's all that matters."

Some would-be great men and women in the Savior's time found it too difficult to continue in faith and hope. Jesus had been discussing the principles of the gospel, and "many therefore of his disciples, when they had heard this, said, This is an hard saying; who can hear it?

"When Jesus knew in himself that his disciples murmured at it, he said unto them, Doth this offend you? . . .

"But there are some of you that believe not. . . .

"From that time many of his disciples went back, and walked no more with him." (John 6:60–66).

Then Jesus asked of his chosen Twelve, "Will ye also go away?" Peter responded with a question that should be meaningful to all of us: "Lord, to whom shall we go? thou hast the words of eternal life" (John 6:67, 68).

Where are we going to go for faith and hope? To our mansions, closets, cars, or jewelry boxes? To our careers, our talents, our accomplishments—shall we go there for hope? What about our good looks, our friends, our passions, our sins—will any of these things give us hope? To whom shall we go for the hope of eternal life?

It was Easter Sunday. The family home evening lesson was on the resurrection, so my conversation turned to the three degrees of glory. I told my family I wanted to go to the celestial kingdom. It was the most important thing to me. Then Steve said, "Me too. I hope—expect—to go to the celestial kingdom, too. In fact, that's the whole reason your mother and I got married. We wanted to go to the celestial kingdom, and we knew we could help each other get there." Ashley voiced the same desire, and then Chase said his goal was to get to the celestial kingdom. All this time, Paige, who was then five years old, looked concerned. Finally she blurted out, "Wait a minute, everybody. I want to go too, but I don't know where it is!"

Steve picked her up and explained one of the names of the Savior. "Paige, none of us knows where it is really. That's why we have to follow Jesus. He knows *the way!*"

"I am *the way*" (John 14:6; italics added). He is *the way* to hope and faith and peace. He is the way home, even home to eternal life.

"Wherefore, ye must press forward with a steadfastness in Christ, having a perfect brightness of hope, and a love of God and of all men. Wherefore, if ye shall press forward, feasting upon the word of Christ, and endure to the end, behold, thus saith the Father: *Ye shall have eternal life*" (2 Nephi 31:20; italics added).

Pressing forward is to push against the adversity of life with courage and determination to succeed. We cannot press forward without a steadfastness in Christ, because that steadfastness makes us resistant and resilient to the forces pressing against us. Steadfastness in Christ comes from the willingness and humility to put our lives into his hands, to seek and to do his will. As we *press* forward to do that, we become more and more obedient. We love God more and we worship him more. We serve him. In serving him, we serve and love others. This love of God and of all men increases our capacity to love ourselves, have hope in ourselves, in others, in all God has planned for us. Love illuminates our lamps of hope. Feasting upon the word of Christ nourishes that light and enables us to endure to the end with a "perfect brightness of hope." And what is the one great hope we have? It is to inherit the celestial kingdom—to have, as the Father said, eternal life.

Eternal life does not mean immortality. Everyone will be resurrected and have immortality. Eternal is one of God's names. Eternal life is to have the kind of life God has. It is to inherit all that the Father has. But it is much, much more even than that. It is to become like Jesus Christ—to possess every attribute, every sympathy, every quality, every bit of divinity possessed by the Savior himself. It is to be all that we struggle and stretch to be in this life—and more. It is to be free from the pains and chains of weakness and to be full of the love of God. It is the greatest hope there is.

I have been developing hope through no ordinary means. I say that only because now, looking back over the past five years, I see how the Lord has provided his children with what seem ordinary but are actually available and accessible tools that bring us power. I am an ordinary woman, but I have had some extraordinary moments, not in spite of my sorrows, but because of them. Mine has not been a life free from sorrow or hardships or heartbreak or challenge. There have been mountains, perhaps even mountain ranges, of doubt. But in my limited years on this earth, spiritual direction in full force has come directly from the gospel of Jesus Christ. The hope in my life, and the degree of its brightness, have come because my trials and challenges have taught me the gospel of our Savior.

A few months ago my husband and I were discussing an unfolding serious situation. He commented about how stressful life is, to which I replied, "You know, I've had a really hard life." He said, "No, you haven't." Surprised, I recounted to him what he already knew. My childhood was not a happy one. Mine was a dysfunctional family. There was extreme emotional abuse. As a teenager I was troubled and rebellious. My attitude was as bad as my choice of friends. I was overweight and ungraceful and ill at ease around others. Because I couldn't sing, dance, or play any musical instruments, I felt untalented. I didn't have a sense of the Lord's love for me because of the abuse at home. Instead, God seemed a hard and unyielding taskmaster. An enormous mountain of doubt overshadowed my knowledge of him and a belief in myself.

There was the turbulent first marriage, the divorce, the low self-esteem, the struggles as a single parent, the years of spiritual apathy, the many mistakes.

Then there were the trials Steve and I have faced in the fifteen years we have been married. There have been great problems in the extended family. These problems have resulted from strife and envy from some family members. One of our loved ones was excommunicated. Several family members have been divorced, one has been an unwed mother, two nieces have come to live with us because of trials they had. There has even been sexual abuse in one of the families and criminal proceedings to deal with.

There have been our own family problems as well. Someone embezzled from us, and there have been other small and great tragedies. I ended the summation of hardships with our greatest sorrow and mountain of doubt, the alcohol and drug addiction of our oldest child.

Steve replied, "When you say it all together like that, yeah, you sure have had a tough life. But I never think of you like that because you're so happy."

I said, "Yes, but it hasn't been a *tough* life. I said a *hard* life. (It's hard work to climb mountains.) But I *am* happy, and its because of the gospel and the hope it brings to me."

Who would ever have believed such a rebellious girl as I was would one day be speaking and writing about looking for the goodness in ourselves and others? Who could ever have imagined then that one day this same girl would be able to exercise hope for a wayward son and have hope in the human heart? Maybe I can see so much hope because once I had to struggle so hard and look so deep to see it in myself.

On March 3, 1985, my son left home forever. He was only sixteen, and I wasn't ready to let go. But the Holy Ghost told me that day to brace myself. My son would never again live at home with the rest of us. It had been a year of struggling to help rehabilitate him from drugs, but now he no longer would allow that. He left us behind, shattered and brokenhearted, when he went away to embark upon five years of hell.

I also was about to face some of the darkest hours I've ever known and begin my journey across a mammoth mountain range of doubt. The horror unfolded in the years that followed. He was arrested many times, beaten, stabbed twelve times and left to die in an alley. We did not know where he was or even if he was alive for a year or more at a time. The spiritual direction that came from the principles of the gospel of Jesus Christ helped me find a path through that mountain range of doubt. So when the call for help finally came, we were able to make it through to the end with a "perfect brightness of hope."

In November he called and pleaded to come home. He asked if we would help him. This time it was real. Under inspiration we were guided to send him to a wilderness survival program. During the sixty days he was gone, everyone encouraged us but told us to be prepared for setbacks. The most we could hope for, we were told, was to get him free of drugs. We were cautioned not to place our hopes too high for any spiritual change.

But after five years of mountain climbing, we were strong enough to hope for—expect—the maximum. With a perfect brightness of hope we as a family spent those sixty days pleading with the Lord for Jason not only to face himself and become drug free but also to be filled with a desire to go on a mission.

The door was opened, Jason had a spiritual experience as had Alma or Enos, and his heart was changed. He returned home in January, received his patriarchal blessing in February, was made an elder in May, received his endowment in August, and in September, on his twenty-second birthday, he entered the Missionary Training Center.

Hope is not a passive emotion that pretends troubles don't exist. It is the belief that they will not last forever. It is the trust that hurts will be healed and difficulties overcome. It is the faith that a source of strength and renewal lies within us to give us direction out of the darkness. It is the expectation that in pursuing that direction we will find a perfect brightness of hope. It is the realization that in that brilliant view we will see the Savior beckoning, "Come, follow me." It is the feelings of love we receive from him as he individually ushers us to the very gates of eternal life.

Chapter Two

Ye Must Press Forward

Whether we lose hope in ourselves or in someone we love because of afflictions, or weaknesses and mistakes, or because of great tragedies in our lives, the emptiness and pain of hopelessness cast darkness over everything we try to do.

Hopelessness feeds the fear of never being able to conquer a sin, of never being able to feel self-control, of never being able to endure the sorrow. Hopelessness fosters a false sense of necessity to give up on ourselves, a loved one, or the Lord. Hopelessness breeds fear and apathy.

Hopelessness comes from hell and the ruler of that sorrowful place. Satan desires our souls and seeks them.

In our striving daily to overcome the "natural man," we are vulnerable to Satan's power, which is subtle and deadly. He may use our very thoughts to discourage us and cause great doubt to fill our souls.

Satan's power to "bruise [our] heel" (Moses 4:21) meant he would have the power to bruise the work of the Lord. He could even influence those who were once loyal to Jesus — as

Judas was. Using his power to bruise, Satan attempts to undermine the covenant people. Some of us are tempted away with sins of commission. But many more of us are discouraged with sins of omission. Sins of omission include neglecting to press forward. When we become apathetic, when we do not press forward, we are subjected to his powerful messages. One of his favorites is "everyone but you has their life in order!" When we allow the devil to persuade us, even through our own hearts and thoughts, to doubt and then to stop believing in ourselves and the Lord (or another one we love), we experience hopelessness. We may be overwhelmed by a feeling that we will never be able to make it to the celestial kingdom.

But we have been given a greater power. When Satan and his followers were given power to bruise our heels, the Savior and his followers (that includes us) were given power to "bruise [his] head" (Moses 4:21). This power also comes through our own hearts and minds. It is the power to press forward, to *choose* to press forward. It is the power to rise up, again, and again, and again. It is the power to obey, to sacrifice, to learn, to serve, and to love.

Can you picture yourself trying to walk against a windstorm? That is what Nephi meant when he said we must press forward. A principle of physics applies here. We cannot *press* forward unless there is an equal force pressing against us. Developing a perfect brightness of hope is like walking against the wind. To press forward is to *choose* to walk against the onslaught of adversity and the day-to-day business of living and struggling in this imperfect world. If we *choose not* to walk against the winds of adversity, then we are unpressing, or depressing. This world is sick to death with depression and hopelessness and faithlessness because most will not "press forward." Entire countries are enslaved in poverty because cultures have taught the people that their station in life is destiny, that how things are is the way God wants them.

Many today have the attitude that we are born a certain way, that it takes a long time to change, and that change is unlikely. A very troubled man in a ward we used to live in came to see Steve and me for some comfort and advice. He and his wife had been having problems, and she had finally contacted an attorney to start divorce proceedings. He had never hit her, but his verbal abuse had been just like hard-hitting blows. Nevertheless, he really loved his family and wanted to succeed with them. Over the past few years he had gone to counseling many times with them. Now he sat in our living room feeling complete hopelessness. He said, "I've learned that I am an abuser. Once an abuser, always an abuser — the best you can hope for is to get it under control. I can't seem to get it under control."

This kind of thinking is meant to stop us from "pressing forward." It is full of hopelessness. It has no place in the hearts of the sons and daughters of God. It is Satan-inspired and Satan-induced. My husband replied to this man, "If that is true, then you are saying that there are Gods out there in the universe who are abusers; they've just got it under control!"

We are free to act and not be acted upon: "Men are free according to the flesh; and all things are given them which are expedient unto man. *And they are free to choose liberty and eternal life,* through the great Mediator of all men, or to choose captivity and death, according to the captivity and power of the devil" (2 Nephi 2:27; italics added). Lehi taught Jacob that "there is a God, and he hath created all things" — "things to act and things to be acted upon" — but of all God's creations, men are "to act for themselves and not be acted upon" (2 Nephi 2:14, 26).

The book *Man's Search for Meaning,* by Victor Frankl,

describes his life in a Nazi concentration camp. His parents, brother, and beloved wife were executed in the ovens. In that house of horrors he came to appreciate free agency:

"What about human liberty? Is there no spiritual freedom in regard to behavior and reaction to any given surroundings? Is that theory true which would have us believe that man is no more than a product of many conditional and environmental factors — be they of a biological, psychological or sociological nature? . . .

"Man can preserve a vestige of spiritual freedom, of independence of mind, even in such terrible conditions of psychic and physical stress.

"We who lived in concentration camps can remember the men who walked through the huts comforting others, giving away their last piece of bread. They may have been few in number, but they offer sufficient proof that everything can be taken from a man but one thing: the last of the human freedoms — to choose one's attitude in any given set of circumstances, to choose one's own way" (*Man's Search for Meaning*, New York: Washington Square Press, 1984, p. 86).

From the beginning 'of this dispensation we have been taught: "For behold, it is not meet that I should command in all things; for he that is compelled in all things, the same is a slothful and not a wise servant; wherefore he receiveth no reward.

"Verily I say, men should be anxiously engaged in a good cause, and do many things of their own free will, and bring to pass much righteousness;

"For the *power is in them*, wherein they are agents unto themselves. And inasmuch as men do good they shall in nowise lose their reward" (D&C 58:26–28; italics added).

In the same way most of us learn the important lessons in life, I gained my deep appreciation of agency, this precious, protected, private gift, from my greatest sorrow. Only as a suffering parent, watching a most beloved firstborn child abuse his agency and die spiritually did I come to understand God's deep commitment to agency, the eternal principal of power and true greatness. With new appreciation I began to see the suffering of our heavenly parents as one-third of their spirit children left heaven, never to return again. I imagined our heavenly parents clutching each other, weeping sorrowfully, as they let their children choose. They had the power to stop them, but they refused to coerce them, because our heavenly parents, as gods, are perfect.

Agency is the key to the plan of salvation — without agency we could never reach our divine potential. How could we? If there were no agency and God continually intervened, we would merely be his puppets, subject to his every whim, submissive only for his good pleasure — and deep down inside ourselves we would know our true condition and feel no strength or power or hope. Elder Neal A. Maxwell has taught:

"Odd, isn't it, how so many mortals denounce or deny God because He will not denounce our moral agency. Yet most human misery occurs because we mortals misuse and abuse our agency. But it's God who gets scolded or denied because of such suffering, when, in fact, as a *long-suffering Father*, He steadfastly supports His plan of salvation in which our agency is the key" (*We Talk of Christ*, Salt Lake City: Deseret Book Co., 1984, p. 24; italics added).

No one feels less personal hope than the person who continually reacts. Persons who usually *react* find their emotional center not within themselves, where it should be, but rather in the world outside them. Whatever the emotional level is around them, they find themselves being raised or lowered by it.

Every criticism, every cross word, every real or imagined

snub plunges the reactor into depression. Every confrontation, every family squabble pushes the reactor to greater levels of frustration. The faintest suggestion of unpopularity clenches the reactor in bitterness. Disappointment, problems, trials, even weaknesses send the reactor on an emotional roller coaster of faithlessness and hopelessness.

Peace within ourselves cannot be achieved until we master our own actions and determine our own attitudes. We cannot achieve our divine potential if we try to solve our problems with drugs or alcohol, profanity, bitterness, sarcasm, self-pity, or apostasy. We came here to this earth, we were born "for such a time as this," to learn how to become more and more like the Master. We came here to learn how to "put off the natural man."

A few years ago I had a telephone conversation with an extended family member, a person who has reacted most of her life. The purpose of her call to me was to inflict injury. The words fell upon my ear with cruel, calculated, trigger-ready action.

I knew clearly what was unfolding. Patience should have been my watchword. My relationship with this person is important enough for me to always hope, "This time it will be different."

It wasn't. The comments stung, caustic words meant to wound, and *I reacted.* I spoke sharply, harshly, impatience ruled, and she hung up.

Then came those warm salty tears that wet the cheek and drench the soul. Not tears of self-pity but tears of struggle — I felt remorse for reacting and I felt the need to repent, but at the same time the sting of the wound stirred my hostility.

A few days later, one of my dear friends who has a degree in psychology talked with me. I told her how intense the incident had been for me, wanting to repent, to not allow myself to get away with it, yet feeling resentment with equal force and wanting justification.

She knows the full background of this relationship and her excellent credentials allowed her to make an accurate and credible statement: "Anita, the relationship being what it is, a powerful one, it is only *natural* for you to feel like this. It is a *natural* human reaction." That answer was satisfactory to me, and that night I comforted myself with thoughts of my natural behavior.

In the predawn hours of the next morning this loving but firm reproach awakened me:

"For the *natural* man is an enemy to God, and has been from the fall of Adam, and will be, forever and ever, unless he yields to the enticings of the Holy Spirit, and *putteth off the natural man* and becometh a saint through the atonement of Christ the Lord, and becometh as a child, submissive, meek, humble, patient, full of love, willing to submit to all things which the Lord seeth fit to inflict upon him, even as a child doth submit to his father" (Mosiah 3:19; italics added).

To become great men and women of faith and hope is to become more and more submissive, more and more like the Savior. Using our agency to become more patient, humble, meek, and full of love, using our agency to be agents unto ourselves and not reactors, is to use our agency to "put off" the natural man.

In his whole life, the Savior taught us by his actions, not reactions. Even when he was personally assaulted he never acted defensively or allowed himself to retaliate. He taught: "He that hath the spirit of contention is not of me, but is of the devil, who is the father of contention, and he stirreth up the hearts of men to contend with anger" (3 Nephi 11:29).

Here is a guideline to help you know if you are acting or reacting: *Act* — you decide what is the right thing to do. You think it through for a few moments. The decision is accompanied by feelings of peace, order, self-esteem, and hope. Then you take positive action. *React* — the clear-cut line between right and wrong is missing. You become confused and mixed up. You can't tell if your response is right or not. You feel you don't know how to handle your problems. Reaction is accompanied by anger, frustration, confusion, and hopelessness.

Agency is the key to our salvation. We can choose to exercise control over our actions when we deal with others, with our environment, and with ourselves in overcoming our weaknesses. This is one of the greatest sermons about hope:

"And if men come unto me I will show unto them their weakness. I give unto men weakness that they may be humble; and my grace is sufficient for all men that humble themselves before me; for if they humble themselves before me, and have faith in me, then will I make weak things become strong unto them" (Ether 12:27).

What comforting doctrine these verses contain! Could it be that we are given weaknesses in the very place we are expected to excel? "I give unto men weakness that they may be humble. . . . If they humble themselves before me, and have faith in me, then I will make weak things become strong unto them." But to become strong we must use our agency to choose to go to the Lord with faith and hope — expectation — that he will reveal us to us. He will allow us the experiences that help us change.

A faithful man, a good friend, over the years has been a silent witness to the truth of this doctrine. As a teenager and young adult he was selfish and self-absorbed. His need to have fun and to have "things" turned into a motivation to steal. He was soon breaking into houses and robbing them. He was eventually caught, tried, and sentenced to prison.

During his incarceration he began to sense his great weaknesses. He began to feel hopeless. Then his thoughts turned to the question, When had he been really happy? He recalled the family home evenings, the Sundays at church and home, the Aaronic Priesthood outings, and like experiences. Those were the times when he had been happy. Slowly, over the course of a few months, he began to change, and a desire to be a part of something better began to grow in his heart.

On his release he began to use his agency to make correct choices. He enrolled in college, he got an honest job, he supported himself. But the emptiness was still inside. The weakness he saw in himself was a hopeless and lonely feeling.

He began to call upon the Lord. A desire to repent fully took hold. He asked the Lord to reveal his weaknesses to him so that he could change. The Lord answered his prayers, and among the thoughts that came to him was the prompting to go on a mission. This young man knew he needed to go. He served a successful two-year mission, married in the temple, has a beautiful family, and has remained active in the Church, even holding responsible Church callings. What his family and others see in him as his greatest strengths are his integrity and honesty. They told me of how once he wouldn't even keep a dime returned accidentally in a pay phone.

I'm certain this individual continues to go to the Lord often, seeking the instruction and counsel necessary to turn a weakness into a tremendous strength. What renewed hope he has found.

Another of my friends has been gaining more self-confidence because of her willingness to seek the Lord's help in overcoming her lack of confidence. Recently she told me he revealed to her that one thing she was doing wrong was going around saying, "I have no confidence." That realization was very exciting to my friend. It was so obvious a mistake but one she had never realized. I've watched her grow over the last few years, gaining confidence and strength — not in spite of her weakness but because of it. Her paying attention to the Lord's counsel and trying to "overcompensate" have made progress happen. Hope is present now as she radiates confidence and poise and trust in the Lord.

Some myths have caused a lot of people to lose hope.

Myth 1: It takes a long time to change. This myth is just not true. Many people change overnight. It doesn't make any difference how long we've been the way we are. We can change quickly if we're *willing* to make an effort. When the *heart* is changed, the behavior is changed. Look at Enos in the Book of Mormon:

"And I will tell you of the wrestle which I had before God, before I received a remission of my sins. . . . and the words which I had often heard my father speak concerning eternal life, and the joy of the saints, sunk deep into my heart. And my soul hungered; and I kneeled down before my Maker, and I cried unto him in mighty prayer and supplication for mine own soul; and all the day long did I cry unto him; yea, and when the night came I did still raise my voice high that it reached the heavens. And there came a voice unto me, saying: Enos, thy sins are forgiven thee, and thou shalt be blessed. And I, Enos, knew that God could not lie; wherefore, my guilt was swept away. And I said: Lord, how is it done? And he said unto me: Because of thy faith in Christ, whom thou hast never before heard nor seen. And many years pass away before he shall manifest himself in the flesh; wherefore, go to, thy faith hath made thee whole" (Enos 1:2–8).

Myth 2: Unless you know what motivates your behavior, you can't change it. This myth is a great misconception. Millions of experiences go into the development of our personalities. Searching for particular reasons for particular behavior is like searching for needles in haystacks.

Remember Paul on the road to Damascus? The Lord appeared to him and asked, "Saul, Saul, why persecutest thou me?" (Acts 9:4). The scripture doesn't say what Paul's answer was, but I doubt he answered because I doubt he knew why he did it. Instead he asked, "Who art thou?" (Acts 9:5). What a great story of how he changed suddenly and how others were astonished to see the great change in him (see Acts 9:3–22).

Myth 3: It's almost impossible to change (people don't really change). I certainly don't want to be judged by the way I used to behave. Do you? We *do* change. Maybe we don't see it in ourselves, but change comes to everyone, even if it is only a little at a time.

Probably one of the most obvious changes we have seen in others is in the contrast between missionaries' farewells and their homecomings. They go out as boys and girls and come home as men and women. Recently I listened to a young man report on his mission. As I watched this mature and poised spiritual leader, I couldn't help remembering his words at his farewell two years earlier: "I really don't know why I'm going on this mission—I guess it's because my mom is making me go!" This Sunday he stood before us and bore a strong testimony of Jesus Christ and missionary work. For me, that contrast is "a perfect brightness of hope."

Myth 4: It's too late to change ("you can't teach an old dog new tricks"). Nonsense! Our behavior is not fixed in concrete. Years of attitudes and actions do condition us, but behavior isn't physical—it's spiritual. The spirit can change.

A friend in Alabama shared with me the tender story of her father's conversion and baptism. Her mother and brothers and sisters had been active in the Church all their lives. Her father had never objected; in fact, he had often attended meetings and was very supportive. He just wanted no part of a commitment to such an exacting religion. The change came when he was humbled over the death of a son. He was in his eighties when he was baptized and confirmed. We both had tears in our eyes as she described the day he and his family knelt across the altar in the temple and were sealed for all eternity. It is never too late to change.

Myth 5: If you change quickly, it won't last. Remember King Lamoni in the Book of Mormon? He and his wife changed quickly, and the change was lasting. Alma changed quickly, and the change was lasting. So did Paul. So did my son. He had a spiritual experience that lasted about thirty minutes. When it was over, his heart had experienced the "mighty change" (Alma 5:14) and he was changed. He went from drug addict to missionary in eight months. "Impossible!" some would say. But such change is real. Real change comes not through changing our thinking but through changing our feelings. "Have ye received his image in your countenances? Have ye experienced *this mighty change in your hearts?*" (Alma 5:14; italics added). That change of heart can come quickly if we subdue our pride and go to the Lord with our weaknesses in humility. That change can last as long as eternity.

Whether we are fighting hopelessness and faithlessness because of adversity, or personal weakness, or because others have abused their agency, we have the *power* to use our own agency to "press forward." Turning a glimmer of hope into a perfect brightness requires a lifetime of pressing forward. And that will, at times, take great courage.

Stories of our prophets show them to be great men who faced life with courage. I believe the Lord gave us such leaders so we could appreciate what our own humanness can accomplish with the Lord's help. Our prophets' greatness and power have come through their obedience to gospel principles. And they have had the courage to be victorious and stand before us as beacons of hope.

There were hours in President Spencer W. Kimball's life when he felt just like the rest of us, full of inadequacy. When he received his call to the apostleship, he was filled with distress and fear and doubt, the opposite of hope.

"It was just breaking day this Wednesday, the 14th of July. No peace had yet come, though I had prayed for it almost unceasingly these six days and nights. I had no plan or destination. I only knew I must get out in the open, apart, away. I dressed quietly and without disturbing the family, I slipped out of the house. I turned toward the hills. I had no objective. I wanted only to be alone. I had begun a fast. . . .

"My weakness overcame me again. Hot tears came flooding down my cheeks as I made no effort to mop them up. I was accusing myself, and condemning myself and upbraiding myself. I was praying aloud for special blessings from the Lord. I was telling Him that I had not asked for this position, that I was incapable of doing the work, that I was imperfect and weak and human, that I was unworthy of so noble a calling, though I had tried hard and my heart had been right. I knew that I must have been at least partly responsible for offenses and misunderstanding which a few people fancied they had suffered at my hands. I realized that I had been petty and small many times. I did not spare myself. A thousand things passed through my mind. Was I called by revelation? Or, had the Brethren been impressed by the recent contacts in my home and stake when they had visited us, or by the accounts of my work in the flood rehabilitation which reports I knew had been greatly exaggerated in my favor? Had I been called because of my relationship to one of the First Presidency?

"If I could only have the assurance that my call had been inspired most of my other worries would be dissipated. I knew if the Lord had revealed to the Brethren that I was to be one of His leaders, that He would forgive all my weaknesses and make me strong. I knew full well that He knew all the imperfections of my life and He knew my heart. And I knew that I must have His acceptance before I could go on. I stumbled up the hill and onto the mountain, as the way became rough. I faltered some as the way became steep. No paths were there to follow; I climbed on and on. Never had I prayed before as I now prayed. What I wanted and felt I must have was an assurance that I was acceptable to the Lord. I told Him that I neither wanted nor was worthy of a vision or appearance of angels or any special manifestation. I wanted only the calm peaceful assurance that my offering was accepted. Never before had I been tortured as I was now being tortured. And the assurance did not come" (*Spencer W. Kimball,* Salt Lake City: Bookcraft, 1977, pp. 192–94).

Eventually the assurance came, but not without effort and not without loneliness. If at first our prayers don't seem to be answered, we must take courage. Remember that Christ himself cried out, "My God, my God, why hast thou forsaken me?" (Matthew 27:46).

We are warriors in the fight for our lives, our eternal lives. We came here to earth for the striving and for the victory. We cannot allow our sword of hope to be thrust into the furnace of hopelessness, or we will find ourselves with a useless and misshapen weapon.

Helen Keller has always been of great interest to me. What prompted this interest was a picture of her I happened to see in the encyclopedia. It was astonishing to see the look on her face. She did not look blind. There was a sparkle in her eyes, a look of depth, intelligence, and recognition. How could that be? Her sightless eyes reflected something wonderfully alive within her.

As I read books about her works and thoughts and accomplishments, I felt her enthusiasm for life and her great ability to press forward. She was left deaf, dumb, and blind as a toddler because of a high fever. Her life was restricted to the confusion inside the world of her own mind.

The love, care, and efforts of her teacher and friend Anne Sullivan taught Helen to press forward. They were two noble daughters of God climbing a mountain of doubt. Helen could have de-pressed. She could have crippled herself further with self-pity and apathy. But she chose to climb. In that climb to the top she served others and loved the world she could not see or hear. In return, the world loved her dearly.

Helen Keller was responsible for much improvement in life for the blind. She graduated from Radcliffe with honors. She was active on the staffs of many foundations for the deaf and blind. She traveled to underdeveloped and war-ravaged countries and helped establish better conditions for the handicapped. She lectured in America and twenty-five other countries. She aided and comforted servicemen who had been blinded in war. She wrote many books, which have been translated into more than fifty languages. Wherever she went, she brought new hope to thousands of blind persons and inspired millions with her zeal.

Her great attitude to press forward is expressed in something she wrote long ago:

"Whenever one door closes, another one opens. The problem with most people, however, is they never see the open door ahead because they are always looking behind at the one that has closed" (*Thoughts from Helen Keller,* Carnival Press, 1968, p. 88).

The Prophet Joseph Smith had years of hardship and tests. There were trials almost beyond our ability to realize. He was tarred and feathered, scorned and abused, even by his closest friends. He had buried loved ones, including his own children. After being beaten, tortured, dragged through streets, even imprisoned, this great man still wrote, on September 6, 1843:

"Now, what do we hear in the gospel which we have received? A voice of *gladness!* A voice of mercy from heaven; and a voice of truth out of the earth; glad tidings for the dead; a voice of gladness for the living and the dead; *glad tidings of great joy.* How beautiful upon the mountains are the feet of those that bring glad tidings of good things, and that say unto Zion: Behold, thy God reigneth! . . . giving line upon line, precept upon precept; here a little, and there a little; giving us consolation by holding forth that which is to come, confirming our *hope!* Brethren, shall we not go on in so great a cause? Go *forward* and not backward. *Courage,* brethren; and on, on to the victory!" (D&C 128:19, 21, 22; italics added).

Look for a moment at the life of my friend Hertha Hales. She was a wife, the mother of six children, and stake Relief Society president when she discovered she had malignant breast cancer. How easily it would have been to slip into hopelessness, especially when doctors said they had done all they could do. But Hertha chose to follow a path lighted by a perfect brightness of hope. Not that she counted on being cured. She wanted that, but she wanted even more to put her life in the Lord's hands. She wanted victory. It did not come easily. It took all the courage she could muster. You can feel her hope in this letter she wrote to me August 31, 1989:

"I finished up my chemotherapy January 1st. I was starting to get worried about having to go to the hospital. So the next night when I had my regular monthly interview with our Stake President, I asked for a blessing. The blessing was given by his counselor, who is one of the most 'spiritually intense' men in our stake. After he gave me the blessing, he was just shaking. He said, 'Those were not my words; they were the Lord's.' The stake president concurred with him. It was a most marvelous blessing and I recorded what I could remember of it—but the three things that I need to tell you about were these: 1. At the beginning I was told three times in three different ways to have faith; 2. I was told twice I still had important things to do on this earth; 3. I was blessed that through me the doctors would be guided. . . . My surgeon had been reluctant to biopsy because it had been his experience that biopsies didn't heal well in this situation. He finally did a needle biopsy and took a frozen section to the lab. When it came back, the report said it wasn't cancer. They said they'd culture the cells and do a further report. When I called in for the results a couple of days later they said they had called in a second pathologist to look at things. At that point I began to wonder. The next day my doctor called and asked if I could meet with him and the surgeon in his office the next day—I knew it must be bad news.

"They told me that it was a recurrence of my breast cancer but the cells had changed. It was now inflammatory breast cancer (a very rapid-growing, bad kind). By this time my whole breast and down into my ribs a little ways were red. The surgeon told me that everywhere there was red skin there were cancer cells and that they couldn't operate because there wouldn't be enough skin to cover the wound. I could see he was right. I asked, 'What are my chances?' He said, 'one in four.' They decided to try to shrink the tumor with chemotherapy and told me they would start the next day. I managed to keep my cool in the doctor's office but as soon as we got out I just fell apart. I was an absolute basket case! It was one of the darkest evenings of my life. Well, I knew I couldn't live my life in tears all the time, and I decided the only thing that could drive the tears away would be the peace of the Holy Ghost. So that night I prayed really hard to be able to have the Spirit.

"The next morning they sent me for lung X-rays and a bone

scan. I was still pretty weepy. Then that afternoon, as I met with the doctors I could feel the Spirit 'kick in,' and I suddenly became calm and peaceful. . . . They started me on the chemo with a little different drug routine than I had last time. That night I got sick. It lasted for about 12 hours before I finally got it controlled. The doctor said we should see some rather dramatic improvements in the breast if the chemo worked. Oh, I need to mention that my doctors both said they had never seen inflammatory breast cancer as a recurrence – that's why they were so stumped at first. I was trying really hard not to be mad at them and to realize they had done their best. After all, they were the top cancer doctors in Idaho.

"We decided to call a special fast. We called our friends and relatives around the country. Several of the wards in our stake fasted, and the high council and stake presidency fasted. At the end of our fast the high council had a special meeting and invited us. Testimonies were shared and President Horward offered a beautiful prayer. The Spirit was very strong there, and I was able to be completely calm and at peace and not cry at all. The next night was Education Week and I was sitting in class and discussing several sections of the Doctrine and Covenants including the 76th. *I got the distinct impression that my Heavenly Father loves me very much and wants very much for me to make it back to the celestial kingdom with him. He was giving me these experiences so I could learn the things necessary to come back and live with him. That was a great comfort!*

"Well, I wish I could have kept the Spirit as strong as it was that week but it's so hard. The next week I could see that my breast was no better and my faith started to waver. I thought, How can I have hope? My third week since the chemo treatment has to qualify as one of the most discouraging of my life. Not only was my breast not getting better, but I could see the red spreading to new areas. . . .

"Going on at the same time was my struggle for faith and hope. It is so hard to have faith when you see your body getting worse every day and the pain getting worse. All I could keep coming back to was the blessing I had been given that said I had things to do on earth, still. How can I believe? I thought. I went back to the blessing again — three times I had been told to have faith. That was the answer — I must have faith that even though things looked terrible now, it would be OK in the end. I thought, Maybe my faith is being taken to the brink to be tested. Then I thought of the great examples in the scriptures. Abraham, when he was asked to sacrifice his son, had faith, even though his hand was not stayed by the Lord until the very last minute. His faith had been tested to the brink. I thought of the children of Israel when they were told to cross over the Jordan River to the promised land. They had to get the soles of their feet wet, before the Lord parted the waters. I thought of them as they marched around Jericho each day — I'll bet on the sixth or seventh day those walls looked just as strong as the first day — and yet they had faith and did as the Lord said and at the last minute the miracle happened. That was my answer then. I must have faith that the miracle I needed would happen."

Hertha was led to a team of doctors at UCLA who performed a type of surgery that would prolong her life. At this point she learned the cancer had spread to the sternum. Her closing comments in the letter are inspiring words of a "perfect brightness of hope":

"As for me, I have had to develop faith that the promises of the Lord unto me will continue to be fulfilled and *hope* that I can complete what I have yet to do on this earth. I thank the

Lord for my life and pray that he will let me know what those things are I have yet to do. My life is in his hands."

Hertha died about eight months later. The miracle never came—or did it? Hertha was able to find out things about herself she had never before known. She learned that she was a woman of faith and hope. But most important of all, she learned that God loves her and that she would put the Savior first in her life, no matter what. She learned that in the end, whatever happened, it would be all right. That is a perfect brightness of hope. Was Hertha defeated? No! She pressed forward with courage and hope, and "on, on to the victory!" She was victorious, after all.

I heard from another woman who struggled for hope in the face of her own sins and excommunication. Through a change of heart, obedience, and the power in choosing right, she was rebaptized:

"Things are definitely progressing here. So many areas of my life are in the process of change—some I haven't even been aware of, until circumstances arrive and decisions are made, easily and correctly.

"I ran across something the other day: 'Christ is the power behind all change.' How true it is. Otherwise, I would be an absolute failure. For he knows I didn't have, and still don't have, any strength in and of myself. I believe that because of *obedience* I am in the process of changing so completely as to gain that inner strength and to receive his will.

"How grateful I am that he made a way back for me, and He pleads on my behalf. How grateful I am for this gospel and the power of free agency and obedience. How thankful I am to being closer to spiritual freedom. I love this scripture, 'God has delivered me from prison, from bonds, and from death; yea, I do put my trust in him, and *he will still deliver me.* And I know that he will raise me up at the last day, to dwell with

him in glory; yea, and I will praise him forever.' (Alma 36:7–
28) I have *hope* again in myself and what I can become."

This woman's struggles are not over. She did not write of
the "press behind" her—she wrote of the "press forward."

I am grateful for the examples around me of persistence
and loyalty to purpose. Individuals who do what God wants
them to do strengthen each of us to do what we should!

Hope has come to me as I have had to remove doubt from
my life, even mountains of it. But I came upon a mountain that
was bigger than all the rest, and I wondered, can I climb it?
Can I truly press forward?

On a spring afternoon in 1985 came the darkest moment
I have ever lived through. My deepest sorrow and agony and
personal suffering had come as I helplessly watched my oldest
son choose to die spiritually. I had felt helpless, but until that
afternoon I had never felt hopeless. Now, alone in my room,
even though the spring day was filled with sunshine, my
thoughts grew darker and darker. Realizing what was happening, that Satan was pulling me down into the furnace of hopelessness, I slipped off my bed and began to pray. Unfolding to
the Lord all the times I had been of good cheer and had endured
continually with faith only let loose the rush of hot tears. Then,
slowly, the question that I had avoided and denied for so long
began to form upon my lips: "Heavenly Father, how can I have
the ability to influence thousands but not my own son?"

In the agonizing silence that followed, my thoughts were
guided to agency. I understood my child's responsibility in
choosing good over evil, but now in this vulnerable moment
I pondered my part in all of it. Into my thoughts flooded all the
moments when I'd yelled, screamed, slapped, and reacted.
Slowly another painful question formed: "Heavenly Father, why
did you send him first, to a young mother struggling herself,
when I am much better equipped to rear him now?"

Somehow, in the moments that followed, it became clear to me I was of no benefit to my son in the condition I was in. He needed my hope, my special gift of hope. So finally a third and final question formed: "Father, will you please strengthen me for the coming hour, until I can stand it again?"

Distinctly, the sweetest voice called me by name and said, "Anita, if I didn't know you could be *victorious*, I would not leave you here."

The glimmer of hope returned.

What I learned in that moment was that the trial was not going to go away yet, but that the Lord knew me and my heartache and had not left me alone. He *was* with me, but he also had some things for me to learn. I needed to discover my own inner victory and do so by developing a perfect brightness of hope.

Several days later two of the questions I had asked were answered. One answer was a letter from a mother whose daughter I had written to. She thanked me for writing books and helping her daughter with a personal note. She concluded her letter by saying she knew of my heartache with one of my children and bore her testimony to me of the law of the harvest. As I have helped water seeds that other mothers have planted, so would there come into my child's life those who would water the seeds in his heart that I had so carefully planted. The glimmer of hope grew brighter.

The second answer came when my visiting teacher talked about children being unable to refuse a mother's gifts. And then she assured me that I now possessed powers to truly help him, not in spite of my own struggles in life, but *because* of them.

But the third witness was the greatest of all. Several weeks later, in a discussion with a relative about some problems in the extended family, I expressed my deep sorrow and concern.

She replied "Don't lose hope, Anita. A line in my blessing says that when my loved ones are called upon to fight the battles of life, they will be *victorious.*" There was the word again, *victorious!* Our Savior would not leave us in a situation unless he knew we could be victorious. Hope burned brighter, and I began my five-year journey, pressing forward, following my son down a road littered with alcohol and drugs. I might have gotten lost in such darkness, but because of the gospel, my way was lighted with a brightness of hope.

Near the end of the apostle Paul's ministry, times grew miserable and burdensome for him. He described his ordeal of being scourged five times with the thirty-nine lashes that often killed the victim; of being beaten with rods; of being stoned and left for dead; of being shipwrecked numerous times; and of his life constantly threatened by his own people, robbers, murderers, and elements, the wilderness, and the sea. He knew he wasn't alone. Many whom he loved, including his friend Stephen, had been slain. I think Paul knew that soon he too would be a martyr. In these conditions, this was his testimony:

"We are troubled on every side, yet not distressed; we are perplexed, but not in despair; persecuted, but not forsaken; cast down, but not destroyed. . . . For our light affliction, which is but for a moment, worketh for us a far more exceeding and eternal weight of glory; while we look not at the things which are seen, but at the things which are not seen: for the things which are seen are temporal; but the things which are not seen are eternal" (2 Corinthians 4:8–9, 17–18).

We are free. Our true freedom has nothing to do with our place of birth, our economic, social, or educational status, or even our nature. True freedom is in our attitude. We have the power to "*choose* liberty and eternal life" — hope — or to "*choose* captivity and death" — hopelessness (2 Nephi 2:27; italics added).

True freedom is a power within. No outward force can destroy it unless we allow it to. It won't happen if we press forward. Whether in a Nazi concentration camp, on the side of a mountain, in a hospital bed in a cancer clinic, or on the wrong end of a flogging, we have the power to press forward toward a more perfect brightness of hope.

Chapter Three

A *Steadfastness in Christ*

The Savior spent his whole life in Galilee. He played there, he ate and slept there, he prayed there. He had made great friends there and also had many loved ones. Galilee was his home, but the course of his life was toward the cross. He was steadfast in following this very course. Nevertheless, when it was time for him to go to Jerusalem, can we even imagine his anguish and the pain of leaving his beloved Galilee and all those he loved so much? But he set for us yet another great example: "And it came to pass, when the time was come that he should be received up, he *stedfastly* set his face to go to Jerusalem" (Luke 9:51; italics added).

He came, he said, to do the will of his Father, and he intended, despite the great personal cost it would be, to do just that. When the appointed hour came in Gethsemane, even the Savior had not anticipated how great the agony would be, as it began to unfold. He grew, it is written, "sore amazed" (Mark 14:33). In the end he submitted totally to his Father's will, he was *victorious,* and he became the Perfect Brightness of Hope for all the world.

Through his submissiveness and humility he was able to remain steadfast in his commitment to carry out the will of his Father. And he had great hope, a perfect brightness of hope, in his Father's love, the plan of salvation, and much more. He had hope—expectation—that many would follow him.

To be steadfast in Christ is to be submissive and full of humility, eager and willing to be a part of his will. The opposite of steadfastness is pride, and pride is a dangerous burden to the brightness of hope.

Pride is the great sin of the spirit.

Pride was the first sin; it was Lucifer's sin. Pride is a deterrent to hope because it keeps us excusing away our negative behavior and attitudes, and procrastinating the spiritual surgery necessary for us to realize the divine potential we really have. Stripping ourselves of pride is a unique unlayering. Instead of removing and discarding a part of ourselves, which is what pride tries to tell us is happening, we soon discover that it is actually an unveiling of the greatness within ourselves. When we see that process happening in ourselves, accompanied by the Spirit, which comes from humility, we are comforted and become full of hope.

President Ezra Taft Benson addressed the Church in April 1989 with a powerful sermon on pride. He spoke like one of the Book of Mormon prophets, warning the Saints to "beware of pride." He cautioned us to be on guard. We see pride often in others but have a hard time admitting it in ourselves. Among some of the ways pride creeps into our lives are gossip, fault-finding, criticizing, murmuring, living beyond our means, envying, coveting, being ungenerous, especially with our love and praise, and being unforgiving and jealous. He named selfishness and contention as "common faces" of pride. He reminded us that the scriptures testify that the proud are easily offended, hold grudges, and do not receive counsel easily. The proud justify their behavior and are not easily taught (see *Ensign*, May 1989, pp. 4–7).

"In the topsy-turvy last days, it is important to realize that as 'the eternal purposes of the Lord shall roll on,' His disciples will surely know what it is to be tumbled. (Mormon 8:22.) It will be no time to be proud, especially when the tumblings may not at the moment seem purposeful. Yet the Lord's work will roll on; His meek disciples will understand.

"Rocks of offense or stones of stumbling keep the proud from making spiritual progress. No less destructive is what might be called the gravel of grumpiness, which keeps us off balance and annoyingly turns ankles. Even though we do not fully fall or stumble, we progress more slowly, painfully, and fitfully. The meek, however, make stepping-stones of stumbling blocks.

"In moments of truth, when meekness matters, other forces, including pride, flow into the chemistry of that moment. Take, for instance, the matter of receiving correct counsel, whether given by a spouse, a family member, a friend, or a Church leader. Often the counsel, even when spoken in love, is resisted by the recipient who—chained by pride—focuses instead upon the imperfections of the person giving the counsel.

"In another situation, the recipient may have much pride in the position he or she has already taken and refuse to deny himself or herself the continuation of that conduct, lifestyle, or attitude *which denial is at the heart of the solution.* However, those who fear losing face cannot have His image in their countenances. (Alma 5:14.)

"In yet another circumstance, the recipient may, instead of listening to the counsel given, be nursing some past grievance upon which he or she would prefer to focus rather than the real issue at hand.

"Whatever the case, experience suggests that recipients of counsel may at the moment of truth feel one or more of these and other restraining forces at work. One force would, by itself, be enough in the absence of meekness, but several combined make meekness crucial. No wonder pride is such a chain! It can be a spreading and encircling chain, 'a root of bitterness springing up [to] trouble you, and thereby many be defiled' (Hebrews 12:15.)" (*Meek and Lowly*, Salt Lake City: Deseret Book Co., 1987, pp. 56–57; italics added).

Pride is unforgiving.

"Wherefore, I say unto you, that ye ought to forgive one another; for he that forgiveth not his brother his trespasses standeth condemned before the Lord; for there remaineth in him the greater sin.

"I, the Lord, will forgive whom I will forgive, but of you it is required to forgive all men.

"And ye ought to say in your hearts — let God judge between me and thee, and reward thee according to thy deeds" (D&C 64:9–11).

I have a friend we'll call Jane. Jane had a best friend she loved like a sister. But the friend had a husband who was proud and abusive and ruled with unrighteous dominion. Jane despised him, because she saw her friend suffer as this man abused his agency. One day he packed up his family and moved them away. Jane lost contact with her dear friend, even though she tried for several years to find her. That only added to Jane's hatred for her friend's husband. Every time she told the story she grew angrier and angrier, and her bitterness increased.

Many years later Jane received a letter from this long-lost friend. The friend also had tried to contact Jane during those years. Finally she met someone who knew Jane and where she was living.

As the letter and the years unfolded, the friend explained about her husband's change of heart. She told of his great sorrow and the process of repentance he had gone through. She told Jane how he had spent the recent years making it up to her. And the most outstanding news? He was currently serving as bishop of their ward.

Jane was stunned. As she began to think about the whole situation, she slowly began to face herself and her own pride. She realized that she had harbored unforgiveness long after her friend's husband had repented and the Lord had forgiven him. She knew then that it was not her place to judge or hold grudges, but of her it was "required to forgive."

The definition of *forgive* is to "lose the desire to punish." When we want someone punished, we want to be justified for the hurt that person has caused us. Harboring such feelings squeezes out the last particle of patience, meekness, and love. Without those, how can we have peace? Unless we are meek and lowly, we cannot feel the Spirit. Without the Spirit, we cannot feel or have true hope.

That is not to say we can't have the Spirit while we are trying to overcome an unforgiving heart. There is a big difference between one who harbors and feeds on unforgiveness versus one who recognizes and is trying to overcome unforgiveness.

A couple in one of my former wards was "offended" by the bishop. They said they wouldn't set foot in the church until he was released. Now, four bishops later, they are still inactive. When questioned about their inactivity, they always refer to that long-ago situation that doesn't even exist anymore. They've lost the Spirit, and they've also lost that brightness of hope that comes with it.

One of my good friends had a great deal of money deceitfully taken from him by a relative. He was angry and filled with the desire to see him punished. He harbored these feelings for years. He still had to have contact with the family member, and it was always stressful. One day he realized that he hated the feelings he had more than he hated the relative. So he began to pray and ask the Lord to help him to remove those feelings and to forgive him for having those feelings. He prayed every day for two years, and every time he got off his knees he felt not one bit better. Then one day he ran into the relative at a store, they exchanged pleasantries, and when he walked away, he noticed he had lost the desire to see this person punished. Those feelings were just gone! He knew the Lord had accepted his efforts and cleansed his heart. The relative was the Lord's to deal with, not his. Most important of all, a sweetness of self-esteem filled his soul. The Comforter reassured him. The weight was gone! He felt peaceful. He felt a renewing of his own spirit. He felt a perfect brightness of hope.

Forgiving someone is like taking a fifty-pound rock off your shoulders. It is a relief, a freedom. Pride keeps the rock in place. The humility needed to forgive and remove the weight does not diminish us; it enlightens us, giving us enough light to have a perfect brightness of hope.

Forgiving others hasn't been easy for me. It took years for me to forgive the person who emotionally abused me. Today there is still no relationship; the person's disdain for me is still alive. The other person hasn't changed, but I have. I love this person now. It isn't easy to be forgiving when we have been hurt, but it feels so much better than being filled with the desire to punish.

When Jason left us, we felt like discarded dirty laundry. The hurt in the other children was, at times, almost unbearable to watch. One night Chase came in my room, sobbing. He flung himself on the bed and pounding his fist into the mattress he wept and exclaimed, "I miss my brother. I can't stand it!" His little seven-year-old heart was swollen with pain. Another time Paige sat for two hours on the front porch, waiting for Jason to come to her birthday party. She was sure he would remember, and no amount of coaxing would convince her to come inside. Of course, he never came, and her eyes hung heavy with disappointment. Ashley hurt so deeply she could not mention his name for two years.

Time after time after time he injured us and inflicted the pain of personal assault, not to mention our sorrow at watching his self-destruction.

I struggled for some time to forgive him. Part of me was praying and hopeful; the other part was angry and resentful. Finally, there came the day I "let go." It was a choice. I chose to let go of the pride in my own hurting heart, and from that moment on my love for him knew no bounds.

We can't change others' attitudes, only our own. It is our responsibility. It is a greater sin to be offended than it is to do the offending (see D&C 64:9–11). This thought continually challenges us to remove pride and seek a sweeter heart. Forgiving someone doesn't remove the burden of repentance from the other person, but it removes the burden of pride and heaviness from our hearts.

Pride is complacent.

"For behold, it is not meet that I should command in all things; for he that is compelled in all things, the same is a slothful and not a wise servant; wherefore he receiveth no reward" (D&C 58:26).

Complacency is a subtle and devious aspect of pride. It insulates us from striving and from changing negative behavior. It encourages us to take the path of least resistance, which is the opposite of what the Savior said. "Take my yoke . . . and learn of me" (Matthew 11:29). "Be ye therefore perfect, even as your Father which is in heaven is perfect" (Matthew 5:48).

A friend who was serving as a Relief Society president in Arizona shared her story of complacency. She had always said, "What you see is what you get" whenever she was confronted with ideas that required her to stretch. Whether those ideas were presented in a lesson, or an interview, or a discussion, she simply used that sentence to insulate herself from any change.

One day she was notified that an elderly single woman who lived in the ward had fallen in a drunken stupor and broken her hip. She was in a nearby hospital and quite alone. The Relief Society president saw her chance for fellowshipping this sister, who had been belligerent. Quickly she organized sisters to clean the elderly sister's house and take care of her pets. She went herself to help and to gather some nightgowns to take to the hospital.

What they found at the woman's home was beyond description. Filth and trash had accumulated for years. There were no decent nightclothes to be found. She decided to purchase a nightgown for the hospitalized sister.

First she went to the hospital for a visit. She found the sister agitated and aloof. The woman was somewhat profane, but the Relief Society president felt that she just needed love and attention. This was the chance she'd been waiting for. This was a chance to help this woman change.

She returned to the hospital the next day with a new nightie, shampoo and rollers, nail polish, and perfume. She greeted the woman cheerfully and began to show her the gifts of love she had brought. The woman got up on one elbow, took the Lord's name in vain, and said, "What you see is what you get!"

This was a turning point for the Relief Society president.

She had seen the need to try to help this woman change, only to be greeted by the very expression she herself used so frequently. She began to see that the Lord had often tried to bring her gifts of love, to help her see more potential in herself, only to hear her say, "What you see is what you get!" This realization changed her life. She removed her complacency, and now hope burns brighter.

One of my brothers-in-law is not complacent about anything. He had recently joined the Church when my sister met him and brought him home to meet us. I remember the enthusiasm he radiated when he shared with me something from a blessing. He said he had been promised that the gospel would help him grow until he became like a polished diamond. He had been a hippie and a drug user before joining the Church. Now, in the gospel of Jesus Christ he had found a perfect brightness of hope, even the hope of becoming a jewel among jewels.

In the eighteen years I've known him this promise has proven true. He embraces the gospel with all his might, mind, and strength. He is not afraid to go the extra mile—in fact, he often seeks it. He always makes a great effort, not just a good one. That is true of his family life and work as well as his Church callings. Today he is handsome, congenial, loved by many.

He cannot sing a note on tune, not one. He loves to sing, however, and the complacency of pride has never stopped him. He loves the Lord so much he wants to sing praises to him.

Because of his calling with the young adults, he and my sister were recently invited to sing in the young adult choir for stake conference. Pride didn't interfere with this opportunity. Complacency wouldn't stop this sweet man from his first and maybe only chance to sing in a choir. My sister told me how tender it was. He beamed a grin from ear to ear and wiped the tears from his eyes as he stood and sang his heart out. No one noticed how off tune he was. They saw only his love for the Lord, for the youth, and for music. A diamond is known for its light and radiance. Surely, his has come from a "perfect brightness of hope" because he refuses to be complacent.

Pride lures us away from choosing the truth.

"And the Messiah cometh in the fulness of time, that he may redeem the children of men from the fall. And because that they are redeemed from the fall they have become free forever, knowing good from evil; *to act for themselves and not to be acted upon,* save it be by the punishment of the law at the great and last day, according to the commandments which God hath given" (2 Nephi 2:26; italics added).

It is a prideful heart that refuses to use agency correctly. Pride snares souls into believing they are born a certain way, or that circumstances control them, that sin is really okay, or that they can't help themselves.

In another ward we lived in there was a handsome young man in his twenties with whom I was impressed. I will call him Gary. He came to see me a few weeks after Jason left home. He explained to me that he had gone on the 250-mile bicycle trip with the Scouts when we had first moved into the ward. He'd gotten to know Jason on that trip, and he said they were a lot alike. He couldn't put his finger on what it was that was so similar. He said, "I see a lot of me in Jason and a lot of Jason in me. I can't describe what it is, I just see it."

Then he explained that he wondered if Jason's problems were like his (he told me he was a homosexual). I said no, Jason's problem was drugs. He offered me some words of encouragement. There was something I really liked about him.

It saddened me to learn a few months later that he had abandoned everything to join the homosexual community. And that was all there was to that insignificant meeting. Until almost four years later.

We had since moved back to Las Vegas. Early one Sunday morning I was awakened before dawn by the thought, Write to Gary. I just wanted to sleep—please, thoughts, go out of my mind! Again, came the thought, Write to Gary. I was nudged several more times, and then I wondered what I would write to him. Almost immediately the strong impressions were there and they were not mine and it was obvious to me that it was time to get up and write. The letter began with my telling Gary that no one was more surprised than I was to be writing to him, but I knew the Lord had awakened me and the letter that was to follow was from him.

I reminded him of the visit he made about four years earlier. I said, "You were right, you and Jason are a lot alike. You did see a lot of him in you and you in him. But his problem is not drugs and yours is not homosexuality. It is *pride.*"

Then I told him what the Lord had taught me in those four years about pride and how it applied to him. I concluded by also telling him of how much hope there was and how much I felt that. I explained how I could feel the Lord's love for him. He was reaching across eternity to bring Gary home. It was for me an amazing experience.

It took a week to contact his mother. She said how unusual I should send a letter at this time. He had just come home from living in Europe and was in the Los Angeles area in despair. He was trying to make sense of his life. Now I was really excited to send the letter. The timing must be right!

About a month later a letter came from him. He had been shaken by my letter. Although he couldn't understand how I could call *pride* what he called a sexual identity crisis, he had felt the Spirit and believed the words of the letter. He wanted to find out more; he was full of despair and hopelessness. Two months passed and another letter arrived, this one filled with a new spirit. It was full of hope. He had returned home to his parents and was reading the scriptures and meeting with the stake president and his bishop. In the months that followed this young man gained a brilliantly clear vision of his own pride. He realized that although he couldn't understand all the "why," he could understand the "how" to change. That change could only come through humility. Humility brings obedience and "a mighty change in us, or in our hearts, that we have no more disposition to do evil, but to do good continually" (Mosiah 5:2).

Today he struggles like the rest of us with a weakness to guard against. But he is obedient and humble. He keeps that broken heart and contrite spirit by keeping the commandments, by attending the temple every morning before work, and by reading the scriptures. He is a great, great man, and he has great, great hope.

The weekend before Jason called for help I had been prompted to read an ad about a wilderness survival program in Arizona. It was sad to me because it only took youth up to age eighteen. I remember thinking, I wish we had known of this years ago.

On Monday, November 13, 1989, I helped host a luncheon on the temple grounds before the public open house for the Las Vegas Nevada Temple. Coming down the hill that afternoon, I could see the whole valley spread out in front of me. It occurred to me that the Lord was pouring out his blessings on this valley because of the temple. I wondered if there could be a blessing for Jason out there, too. Suddenly the thought came, Wouldn't it be nice if he could go on that wilderness program? What a ridiculous thought! He was too old. Besides, how would we get him there? He would never go on his own, and we didn't even know where he was.

That evening he called, and this time his plea for help was real. We picked him up on a street corner. His only possessions were the clothes he had on. They had been borrowed from a boy who had found him choking to death in his own vomit in an alley. He had taken him home and helped him through the next twenty-four hours. Jason had felt hopeless, and this boy encouraged him to go home.

We were able to send him to Arizona five days later for what was supposed to be an experience to teach him self-reliance and self-control. We at least felt that we had been guided under inspiration and that perhaps out there a "change of heart" could occur. But, not one of us was prepared for the glorious experience that happened, least of all Jason.

As the weeks passed by, the reports were less than encouraging. With hope we prayed fervently day after day, many times a day. Finally the counselors called and said they had done all they could. A spiritual change had not taken place. They had decided that this would be his last week with them. He had already been with them three weeks longer than any other students, and they had done all they could do with him. They were going to put him on "solo" for one week: he would be alone in the Arizona wilderness with a Book of Mormon and a copy of President Benson's talk on pride with a challenge to read them.

When they left him alone on the mountain, he was unhappy about staying the additional week. He was unhappy because all those weeks on the trail had not brought him the peace he was seeking. He decided to take the challenge and read the Book of Mormon. He also began to pray and ask for the feelings of peace and hope to return to him again. He felt nothing. For three days he fasted and read the Book of Mormon and Pres-

ident Benson's talk on pride. He felt empty. He pleaded with
the Lord: why couldn't he feel what he used to feel when he
was at home?

On the fourth morning this is what happened, written in
his own words with the stub of a pencil on a piece of paper
he had with him:

"January 3, 1990 Today I see life from a completely different
angle. I know of a surety that the Lord God does listen and
answer our prayers. Remember they have to be given in faith
and humility. Yesterday I was sitting here next to my fire reading
the Book of Mormon when I decided to go find some more
reeds for my arrows. I walked about 400 yards when I found
some to my liking. I began to cut some down and look at them.
I was very excited. I turned, looked at my camp. It was on fire.
Now I had set my camp between two very big branches of a
tree that had fallen to the earth and died. Next to them was
the very, very large tree they had fallen from. It was winter so
there were many leaves on the ground around my camp. I
began to run back to my camp while in my heart I served up
a prayer to the Lord to help me. Now the wind had never been
so strong in all of the 50 days I was there as it was on this day.
The sky was beautifully blue and the sun was hot. (Not a cloud
in sight.) As I approached my camp I could see the fire was a
rager and it was spreading fast. My first thought was to run to
the power plant which was a good mile as the crow flies, but
then I realized that I was going to be held responsible for it
so I didn't. I picked up a peach can and my little one cup
stainless steel cooking can and ran for the river (about 100
yards from camp) when I returned the large tree was half way
enveloped in flames. I threw all the water I had to the top of
the flames which extinguished them for about 30 seconds. I
repeated this for about four or five minutes until I saw I was
not helping. On the return to the river I collapsed to my knees

from heat and exhaustion. I then began to pray to the Lord to help me control this fire till someone would see it and come to my aid. I got up and ran for the river again. After about 20 minutes of this I began to see that even with the raging winds the fire was being contained to about a 25 to 30 foot by 8 foot range, not including the tree.

"The flames that were climbing the side of the tree began to encircle the whole thing (in circumference about 10 1/2 to 11 feet). I was doomed! I knelt down in the middle of the dry river bed and this is what happened.

"I began to pray to the Lord not knowing that I was in store for the greatest experience of my life. As I began to pray I felt the spirit of the Holy Ghost, a feeling I have not felt for a long time come over my whole being. I began to cry, even to weep greatly. I asked the Lord with all the sincerity of my heart with real and true humility with all my faith in Him that He would send the rain. After praying to him for two or three minutes I got up and ran to the river when I turned around the flames were growing exceedingly big climbing the tree and spreading through the leaves. But for some reason which I know now was the Holy Ghost comforting me, I was calm and at peace. I returned to the river many times to retrieve that half gallon of water and to throw it on the flames. I looked up after a while, I don't remember the time, but there were rain clouds even the whole sky was gray with thick rain clouds. I began to cry and knelt down and praised the Lord for answering my prayers.

"I felt the Spirit bear witness to me that the Lord does live. He does answer prayers and He does love me greatly. It rained all night long and when I got up this morning not a coal was hot from that fire yesterday.

"I sit here this morning and the sun is shining warm. There is no wind. The water in the river is rushing loudly. The birds are singing. The snow is on the mountains and I am feeling the spirit of the Lord again. I love you, Heavenly Father and do not doubt the great being that you are. It feels good to be humble. It feels good not to be proud. It feels good to know I am forgiven.

"I cannot wait to tell everyone I can about the gift of prayer and the gift of repentance and forgiveness."

The first prayer he uttered was for assistance from someone else. The second prayer came from complete humility. He didn't need anyone but the Lord. Jason asked him simply to send the rain. When the last shred of pride was removed, the Lord accepted his prayer and his repentance. Pride, until that moment, had always lured him away from choosing the truth. And like Gary, Jason found the antidote to be humility. He expressed his feelings in a poem he wrote a few hours after his great experience.

> I know now what it was inside
> That made me laugh when people cried
> That made me scoff and scorn at some
> To even tease and poke fun.
>
> I know now what it was about me
> That drove so far away from thee
> That made me slip and loose the rod
> That took me so far away from God.
>
> I know now what it was to hide
> Behind the evil wall we know as pride
> I didn't care about anyone
> To me Jason Brooks was number one.
>
> I know what it was that hardened my heart
> And made me play this wicked part
> After fast and prayer it dawned on me
> I need to find humility.
>
> I knelt down to the Lord and said

Father I humbly bow my head
And offer this prayer I know you'll hear it
I have a broken heart and contrite spirit.

Help me Father with this proud heart of mine
I've been away for such a long time

I know now in the Lord's own way
In a still small voice he did say
Just a few words that hit me like a ton
I love you, welcome back, you're forgiven my son.

When we remove pride, a new spirit is born. Humility brings out the goodness in us. As a witness to that, several months after Jason returned home from the wilderness experience, a counselor called to tell him something incredible. This counselor had hiked up to Jason's solo area. To his amazement, the dead tree that had been engulfed in flames was alive again and in full bloom! He told Jason he could feel the spirit of this place and that the tree was indeed a witness of new life. That is what hope really is all about.

Pride wallows in self-pity.

"For the natural man is an enemy to God, and has been from the fall of Adam, and will be, forever and ever, unless he yields to the enticings of the Holy Spirit, and putteth off the natural man and becometh a saint through the atonement of Christ the Lord, and becometh as a child, submissive, meek, humble, patient, full of love, willing to submit to all things which the Lord seeth fit to inflict upon him, even as a child doth submit to his father" (Mosiah 3:19).

The "natural man" is an enemy to God. The natural part of us feels sorry for ourselves when things go wrong. Pride keeps us from being able to submit to all things that the Lord sees fit to inflict upon us.

One unforgettable person I have met was a young woman with thick pop-bottle-bottom glasses. She was seated in a congregation with a huge pad of paper, like an artist's drawing pad, and a black marker. She was taking notes while the speakers presented ideas. Later she told me she was going blind. All she could see now were huge letters made with a magic marker. She spoke of her bitterness at first, then of her self-pity, and then of her love for God. She felt it would be okay now, that perhaps he had a work for her to do that she could only do blind. Perhaps she needed to learn to appreciate other things. At least, she said, there must be some exciting lessons ahead for her. What humility! She affected me deeply. She showed me a "perfect brightness of hope" through her lack of self-pity.

Pride refuses responsibility for its actions.

Pride likes to blame others. In Alma 61 and 62 is a great example of taking responsibility for our own actions.

It was a time of great war and bloodshed in the land. Moroni had written to the chief judge, Pahoran, for more troops and provisions. He didn't know Pahoran had been removed from the government and had fled to Gideon to enlist more troops to gain back the city. Moroni sent a scathing letter to Pahoran.

"For behold, I have somewhat to say unto them by the way of condemnation. . . .

"But behold, great has been the slaughter among our people; yea, thousands have fallen by the sword, while it might have otherwise been if ye had rendered unto our armies sufficient strength and succor for them. Yea, great has been your neglect towards us. And now behold, we desire to know the cause of this exceedingly great neglect; yea, we desire to know the cause of your thoughtless state. Can you think to sit upon your thrones in a state of thoughtless stupor, while your enemies are spreading the work of death around you? Yea, while they are murdering thousands of your brethren. . . .

"Behold, could ye suppose that ye could sit upon your thrones, and because of the exceeding goodness of God ye could do nothing and he would deliver you? Behold, if ye have supposed this ye have supposed in vain. . . .

"But why should I say much concerning this matter? For we know not but what ye yourselves are seeking for authority. We know not but what ye are also traitors to your country" (Alma 60:2, 5–7, 11, 18).

He concluded by telling Pahoran he would come back and smite them with the sword.

What would have been your reply? Mine probably would have been, "And who do *you* think *you* are? Here I am fighting to stay alive and gain support etc., etc.!" No one would have blamed Pahoran for being upset or angry with Moroni. It would have been natural. Reading the account of Pahoran's struggles makes the reader feel bad that Moroni called him a traitor. What if you had been Pahoran?

Pahoran's reply in meekness and humility is a lesson and example to all of us. It probably was to Moroni as well:

"I, Pahoran, who am the chief governor of this land, do send these words unto Moroni, the chief captain over the army. Behold, I say unto you, Moroni, that I do not joy in your great afflictions, yea, it grieves my soul. But behold, there are those who do joy in your afflictions, yea, insomuch that they have risen up in rebellion against me, and also those of my people who are freemen, yea, and those who have risen up are exceedingly numerous. . . .

"And now, in your epistle you have censured me, but it mattereth not; I am not angry, but do rejoice in the greatness of your heart. I, Pahoran, do not seek for power, save only to retain my judgment-seat that I may preserve the rights and the liberty of my people. My soul standeth fast in that liberty in the which God hath made us free. . . . Therefore, my beloved brother, Moroni, let us resist evil, and whatsoever evil we cannot resist with our words, yea, such as rebellions and dissensions, let us resist them with our swords, that we may retain our freedom, that we may rejoice in the great privilege of our church, and in the cause of our Redeemer and our God. . . . And now I close mine epistle to my beloved brother, Moroni" (Alma 61:2–3, 9, 14, 21).

Had Pahoran been angry and retaliated with sarcasm and like accusations, the country might have perished. It might have lost two great leaders. But because Pahoran was meek and humble and took responsibility for his own actions, words, and feelings, hope returned. The nation rallied under two great leaders and regained its liberty. Many also have been influenced by his example, not only then but now as well.

My sister told me about a friend who showed her a list she was preparing to take to her counselor. It was a page filled with problems and complaints against or about her husband and their marriage. My sister observed, "My marriage doesn't have problems. My husband and I don't have *marital* problems. *He* has problems, and *I* have problems, but the marriage doesn't have problems. If we spend our energy working on our *own* weaknesses, the marriage is just fine!"

What a great example of taking responsibility for our own actions. Pride wants to blame others or make others responsible for how *we feel.* If we *feel* bad inside, it is usually because we have some negative behavior. Our bad feelings are always full of hopelessness and faithlessness. Pride keeps us from facing ourselves and being responsible for ourselves. It is easier and safer to blame others.

Pride likes its own opinion.

Some years ago a book was published that told the story of a man's struggle with homosexuality, written by his wife. Soon I began receiving phone calls from all over asking my opinion. My opinion was not favorable. With each phone call my hostility increased. I was ready, able, and willing to speak out against the book. I even felt resentment toward the author.

The day soon came when I had a Church assignment to fill that would require the full force of the Spirit. The night before I felt empty. Finally I had to ask what was wrong. Why did I feel out of step with the Lord? I told him I'd been distracted all week and asked him please to show me my part in the emptiness.

The thought came to me to read the Book of Mormon. In only a few minutes these verses sank deep into my heart:

"See that ye are not lifted up unto pride; yea, see that ye do not boast in your own wisdom, nor of your much strength. Use boldness, but not overbearance; and also see that ye bridle all your passions, that ye may be filled with love; see that ye refrain from idleness. . . .

"Do not say: O God, I thank thee that we are better than our brethren; but rather say: O Lord, forgive my unworthiness, and remember my brethren in mercy — yea, acknowledge your unworthiness before God at all times" (Alma 38:11–12, 14).

So that was it! Pride in my own opinion. Even through my own strength and wisdom I had been distracted. We can carry even truth past the safe mark, thus the term *self-righteous.* My opinion of the book hadn't changed, but my attitude toward stating it and my attitude toward the author had changed. I had been "overbearing" in that opinion. I needed to use "boldness" combined with love and compassion. I gained renewed hope in myself and the great generosity of God.

When we gossip, criticize, backbite, or murmur, it is pride. We are "lifted up" in our own opinions, our pride. President Benson appealed to us to "beware" of this deadly sin that destroyed the Nephite nation. Because of pride the Nephites eventually lost all hope.

The antidote for pride is humility, which is turning our strength over to the Lord. One important question we can ask the Lord is, "Heavenly Father, will you show *me my* part?" Can you imagine the problems that could be solved, the sins forestalled, the arguments mended, relationships repaired if we each asked the Lord that question—and then listened to and acted on the answer?

A woman fought against her husband's counsel to do her part in mending strained family relationships by going to each family member and saying, "I've had hard feelings toward you. Please forgive me." The counsel was exactly what the Savior would have instructed her to do. But instead of going to the Lord and asking, "Show me my part," she went to others seeking to justify her attitude and her opinion. After amassing a "camp," it was too hard to follow the counsel. Instead of being wrong just in front of the Lord, or a few people, she now would have to be wrong in front of her "camp." It was too hard—she was too full of pride. Her beautiful marriage came to an end. Her pride devoured any brightness of hope.

One of this woman's stepdaughters shared with me some tender insight into this "hopeless" situation. During the course of trying to resolve the problems, this daughter spent several hours with the woman trying to help her understand the gospel principles associated with the husband's counsel. She even went the extra mile in doing her part by asking her stepmother to forgive her of anything she might have done wrong.

It was useless. The woman was so full of pride that she would not soften her hardened heart toward her husband, his children, or anyone who seemed to try to help the situation. This daughter described how she left that home overwhelmed with the spirit of contention she had felt there. She drove away sorrowful because a darkness settled upon her and she knew then that the marriage would end in divorce.

That night the daughter prayed for understanding. She had lost *hope.* She questioned whether or not that was wrong. We are supposed to have hope, to keep hope. What was she feeling? The answer came immediately as the words of a scripture filled her mind:

"For the Spirit speaketh the *truth* and lieth not. Wherefore, it speaketh of things as they *really* are, and of things as they *really* will be" (Jacob 4:13; italics added).

It was clear to her then that she had not simply just "given up" hope but that the Spirit had shown her the truth of things as they really are and really will be. She was greatly comforted and was able to help her father through the grim separation and divorce. Hope was renewed, this time in a most unusual manner, and for different purposes.

The Holy Ghost is the Comforter. He bestows the spirit of hope as we seek that spirit through humility. When humility and meekness are present, so is the Holy Ghost. In all situations where pride is a factor, the Holy Ghost is of great importance.

A lot of people have made mistakes they wish they could change or advice they wish they could reword. A lot of people hate the feelings of unforgiveness they carry. Probably all of us wish we could go back and undo or redo something in our past.

Elder Neal A. Maxwell wrote:

"There are, for instance, a number of words in the scriptures that we assume we know the meaning of, but in our casualness we fail to search them. One such word occurs in the revelation given to the Prophet Joseph Smith in Liberty

Jail. It declares that true leadership requires 'reproving *betimes* with sharpness, when moved upon by the Holy Ghost; and then showing forth afterwards an increase of love toward him whom thou hast reproved, lest he esteem thee to be his enemy.' (D&C 121:43. Italics added.) Most of us casually assume the word *betimes* means 'from time to time,' or occasionally. *Betimes* actually means 'early on.'

"If we both identify a need early and are moved upon by the Holy Ghost to act before pride has hardened our attitudes, we have a greater likelihood of success. Our effectiveness in working with others depends not only upon our meekness but also upon theirs, and mutual meekness is more apt to be present 'early on' rather than later" (*Meek and Lowly*, p. 40).

Enroute from San Francisco to Salt Lake City the pilot told us over the public address system to look out our windows. He said, "Well, there is the Nevada desert, not much to look at, but I wanted you to see it's there!" He then made a few more jokes about the barren land below us. Everyone laughed, including me, even though I've been a desert dweller now for most of my life.

Little did I realize how much this incident would affect me. As the days passed I began wondering, What am I doing in the desert? Why don't we live somewhere else? I began to think about what value there is in such dry and open places.

Of all the places on earth, the desert most nearly represents the kind of person I want to be someday, the true woman in Christ. The desert is stripped of pride but yet is worthy and full of dignity.

The desert has the courage to press forward, to stand between majestic mountains, grand oceans, tropical paradises, refreshing waterfalls, rolling landscapes and forests, and say, "I, too, belong here. I am of great worth. I, too, can contribute. See my value." The desert has the courage to make a contribution without the approval of others.

The desert is valiant. The desert shows the passer-by, This is what I will do, what you can expect from me, what I stand for; and this is what I won't do, what you cannot expect from me. The desert is consistent, like the Savior and his laws.

The desert is submissive. It yields to the scorch of the relentless sun and to the fury of the wind. The desert doesn't wither away nor does it allow itself to be blown into non-existence. It simply submits, and submits, and submits. It submits to nature's shaping without complaint of loss or discomfort. Its echo is the voice of long ago, " . . . not my will, but thine, be done" (Luke 22:42).

The desert is unpretentious and humble. Only the necessities are there. Water is to be found, if you look for it. Shade is there, if you absolutely need it. Whatever doesn't belong or has outlived its usefulness, the great winds simply come along and whip it away.

The desert never pretends to be what it is not. Man comes in to tame it, and it yields to his desires. The desert shows true humility. It is willing to be taught and improved. It never cowers in its inadequacies but concentrates on its strengths.

The desert has earned beauty. It isn't something artificial or superficial. It's not a beauty from something external but rather from something internal. The highs and lows of form and shadow required years of polishing with fine grains of sand. The flowers among the sage and cactus and bristles are true serendipity. They have earned the right to bloom as they have weathered sun and wind and lack of natural vegetation and cultivation. Such flowers are not unlike candidates for the celestial kingdom who endure to the end. The earned glories of the desert are not unlike what the Master has been through.

The sunrises and sunsets in the endless skies above the

desert mirror a beauty not easily seen from the desert floor. The deeply layered colors reflect the desert's inner beauty, inner soul.

It is spiritually significant to me that the Lord chooses the desert to refine his people and strip them of pride. Into the desert he sent Adam and Eve, Elijah, Enoch, Moses and his people, and families of Lehi and Ishmael, and even John the Baptist, who "grew and waxed strong in spirit, and was in the deserts until the day of his shewing unto Israel" (Luke 1:80).

And where did the Savior go to fast and pray and prepare for his ministry upon the earth? He went into the desert.

In our own day the Lord once again sent his people into the deserts of Utah to be refined, strengthened, and humbled enough to build from that place a people that would fill the whole world.

An almost sacred environment surrounds my home in Las Vegas. Outside the casinos, the vulgar billboards, the neon and flesh, the desert is a natural citadel of spiritual strength for this worldly city. Most of its inhabitants don't even know that, or care.

The desert reminds me of who I am and what I am not, of who the Savior is and what I want to be.

We must "press forward" with a "steadfastness in Christ," with the great desire and effort for more humility. Otherwise, we will be engulfed in one form or another of pride. We will find ourselves "proud, knowing nothing, but doting about questions and strifes of words, whereof cometh envy, strife, railings, evil surmisings [suspicions] . . . and destitute of the truth" (1 Timothy 6:4–5). Without the Holy Ghost, we are "ever learning and never able to come to the knowledge of the truth" (2 Timothy 3:7) because the "Spirit speaketh the truth and lieth not" and will show you "things as they really are, and of things as they really will be" (Jacob 4:13).

When the Spirit shows us our weaknesses and "speaketh truth," we know what our part is. When the Spirit shows us "things as they really are," we are comforted and full of hope because we also see things as they "really will be." The Holy Ghost inspires us to improve our thoughts, actions, and attitudes, "for God hath not given us the spirit of fear; but of power, and of love, and of a sound mind" (2 Timothy 1:7).

One beautiful and spiritual young woman learned these principles after her own world had become embroiled in bitterness and hopelessness. She married a returned missionary in the temple and had her life all planned. Within three months her world and her plans were shattered. He admitted that he had been living lies. He was soon excommunicated for some things he had done while on his mission. She felt deceived. Her faith and confidence were shaken. She had been obedient and prayerful all of her life. What was happening, and why? For the next two years, she tried to put her marriage back together without her husband's cooperation or interest. The marriage was a disaster, her faith had been shaken, and she was working several jobs and trying to care for a newborn infant. There was no support or effort from him. She was enticed away from nobility by a co-worker, and she ended up excommunicated as well. She and her husband divorced, and she began a tailspin into hopelessness. She learned firsthand what it was to be without the Holy Ghost and to "have a spirit of fear." She wanted the Holy Ghost back in her life; she wanted again the peace, the love, the power, the sound mind.

So she began her journey back over that mountain of doubt. It has taken time and struggle, but she has made it. Today she is even more beautiful, even more radiant. Here is her beautiful and sincere testimony, written near the time of her rebaptism:

"I have sacrificed precious time given here on earth when I could have been progressing as Heavenly Father would have wanted me to. I feel an urgency to press forward and to do those things that Heavenly Father would want me to do. One of those choices would be to go to the temple. I have missed it greatly—the blessing of service, the blessing of peace, the blessing of renewed covenants and dedication, the blessing and beauty of Heavenly Father's simple yet beautiful plan, the blessing of assisting in the preparation of the church for the Second Coming of Christ.

"I have always known the gospel is true. I have always sustained and had a strong testimony of the authority of the church leaders. I realize the power of prayer, scripture study, revelation, and fasting and the great influence these can have on my life. I have always paid a full tithe and continue to do so. I don't question the moral standards of the church and see through obvious personal experience the importance of following a chaste pattern of lifestyle. I have always attended church when able and want more than anything to continue to follow the principles and ordinances of the gospel always.

"I know the gospel is true. I know that Heavenly Father and His Son, Jesus Christ, live and love us. I know that Joseph Smith is a prophet of God and that through him, Jesus Christ restored His church upon the earth in these latter days to prepare His Kingdom for His return. I know that President Benson is a true prophet of God and guides and directs the church here on earth through revelation as have all the prophets in all the dispensations. I know that the Book of Mormon is true. My wish is to be the Lord's humble and obedient servant to help move His kingdom forth."

Pride simply prolongs the pain of facing ourselves. But face ourselves we must. The longer we delay, the longer we avoid the Spirit of Truth, the greater our fall will be and the longer we have to dwell in darkness and fear instead of with the Perfect Brightness of Hope and the power he brings.

Chapter Four

Feasting upon the Word of Christ

Never have I seen more hopelessness than in the faces and eyes of mothers clutching their dying children in the deserts of Africa. These starving children did not have the strength even to cry in their dying agony. There was no food to save them. Many rescue workers who tried to help in some small way lost their desire to eat. Many went home ill. They had been overcome with the starvation, the disease, the death that occurred even before those pitiful souls drew their last breath. Despair was a thick blanket that smothered any small glimmer of hope.

In a like way there is hopelessness on the faces of many who are starving for truth. In front of us sits a banquet of truth that will not only enhance our hope but cause us to *expect* that we can obtain the celestial kingdom. "Feast upon the words of Christ; for behold, the words of Christ will tell you *all* things what ye should do" (2 Nephi 32:3; italics added). "If ye shall press forward, feasting upon the word of Christ, and endure to the end, . . . ye shall have eternal life" (2 Nephi 31:20).

Feasting means to eat with abundance. Many simply snack at the scriptures and then claim there is no hope in them.

"Feasting upon the word of Christ can provide needed adrenaline for deepening and maintaining discipleship. Joseph Smith called one especially nourishing disclosure (Moses 1) a 'precious morsel.' These disclosures involve more than intellectual calisthenics; they push out the borders of our understanding and can restructure our understanding of ourselves, the world, and the universe, teaching us things we 'never had supposed.' (Moses 1:10.)

"If we will feast upon the gospel's transcending truths and apply them, we will not be 'wearied and faint in [our] minds.' (Hebrews 12:3.) Fainting intellectually will not occur when we are properly nourished. We can have assurances to sustain us that will keep us from fainting in our minds. . . .

"With such intellectual and spiritual nourishment, we can not only rejoice, but, significantly, we will also 'be filled with love towards God and all men.' (Mosiah 2:4.) People fatigue is dissipated by love and learning. . . . Marvelous outcomes flow from inspired insights from the Spirit or scripture. Refreshment, renewal, and reassurance follow. There is also a keener sense, on our part, that we are in fact surrounded 'with so great a cloud of witnesses.' (Hebrews 12:1.) We become a part of a vast community of believers that transcends time and space, providing precious perspective" (*Meek and Lowly,* pp. 41–42).

How exciting to be a "part of a vast community of believers." That thought itself brings hope and comfort; we are not alone.

Soon after Jason left I discovered that the only way I would not "weary and faint" in my mind was to immerse myself in the scriptures. They kept the brightness of hope burning. Never before had Alma's prayer for his son meant so much:

"And again, the angel said: Behold, the Lord hath heard the prayers of his people, and also the prayers of his servant, Alma, who is thy father; *for he has prayed with much faith*

concerning thee that thou mightest be brought to the knowledge of the truth; therefore, for this purpose have I come to
convince thee of the power and authority of God, that the
prayers of his servants might be answered according to their
faith" (Mosiah 27:14; italics added).

Comfort came as I read of Alma the Younger's repentance:

"But I was racked with eternal torment, for my soul was
harrowed up to the greatest degree and racked with all my
sins.

"Yea, I did remember all my sins and iniquities, for which
I was tormented with the pains of hell; yea, I saw that I had
rebelled against my God, and that I had not kept his holy
commandments. . . .

"Oh, thought I, that I could be banished and become extinct
both soul and body, that I might not be brought to stand in
the presence of my God, to be judged of my deeds.

"And now, for three days and for three nights was I racked,
even with the pains of a damned soul.

"And it came to pass that as I was thus racked with torment,
while I was harrowed up by the memory of my many sins,
behold, *I remembered also to have heard my father prophesy
unto the people concerning the coming of one Jesus Christ,*
a Son of God, to atone for the sins of the world.

"Now, as *my mind caught hold upon this thought,* I cried
within my heart: O Jesus, thou Son of God, have mercy on me,
who am in the gall of bitterness, and am encircled about by
the everlasting chains of death.

"And now, behold, when I thought this, I could remember
my pains no more; yea, I was harrowed up by the memory of
my sins no more.

"And oh, what joy, and what marvelous light I did behold;
yea, my soul was filled with joy as exceeding as was my pain!"
(Alma 36:12–20; italics added).

Inspiration came with verses about the love of the Savior for his people, about "his tender mercies" (1 Nephi 1:20), what the Atonement means to all of us. I felt his love and understanding. More power came as I pondered Moroni's sermons on faith, hope, and charity (Moroni 7; 8), and the discourses in the Doctrine and Covenants on spiritual gifts (D&C 46). And in the New Testament the descriptions of the Savior's life and obedience gave me an inspiring example to mark my path.

Hope glimmered at first and then burned brighter with my daily reading of verses such as these:

"But behold, he did deliver them because they did humble themselves before him; and because they cried mightily unto him he did deliver them out of bondage; and thus doth the Lord work with his power *in all cases* among the children of men, extending the arm of mercy towards them that put their trust in him" (Mosiah 29:20; italics added).

Who can resist stretching for hope while reading of the great hope Lehi maintained until the end of his life? It is remarkable that even after seeing in vision his sons Laman and Lemuel refuse the fruit of the tree, he continued to counsel them. He blessed them and prayed for them and even to the end of his life, he never gave up on them (see 2 Nephi 2:28; 4:1–12).

A significant moment of hope came while I was reading the scriptures shortly after I learned that Jason had been stabbed and left for dead in an alley. His life had been saved, and perhaps that would be the turning point for him. Perhaps he would realize how bad his life was and he would come home. As the days turned into weeks and the weeks into months, hope faded to only a glimmer again. Then I read:

"And I will tell you of the wrestle which I had before God, before I received a remission of my sins.

"*Behold, I went to hunt beasts in the forests;* and the words which I had often heard my father speak concerning eternal life, and the joy of the saints, sunk deep into my heart.

"And my soul hungered; and I kneeled down before my Maker, and I cried unto him in mighty prayer and supplication for mine own soul; and all the day long did I cry unto him; yea, and when the night came I did still raise my voice high that it reached the heavens.

"And there came a voice unto me saying: Enos, thy sins are forgiven thee, and thou shalt be blessed" (Enos 1:2–5; italics added).

The words "I went to hunt beasts in the forests" struck me forcefully. Where was Enos when he "hungered" for change? He wasn't at home, or in family home evening, or in sacrament meeting. He was out in the forest. Whether hunting for food or sport, his mind was elsewhere. The "weary and faint" feelings began to dissipate as I "feasted" upon those words. I was excited and grateful again for words of love and encouragement and hope. The brightness returned. But that was not to be the end of this great moment with that scripture.

We put Jason on the plane to go on the wilderness survival program on a Friday morning. We felt it was under inspiration that we had been prompted to send him on this particular program. But as soon as he left we were covered with an overwhelming cloud of doubt. What if this didn't work? What if we hadn't been inspired? Could we stand the heartbreak again? What if he straightens out but won't have anything to do with the Church? What if we're asking the Lord too much in asking that he can be inspired to go on a mission? This was going to cost a lot of money. What if he runs away? What if he fails? Can he stand yet another failure? Can we?

For two days we were tormented. We see now it was Satan distracting us away from a perfect brightness of hope. Hope was needed in order for us to pray with power for him.

Saturday evening I retired early and reaffirmed my faith in the inspiration to send him, asking to be strengthened so that I could be the maximum spiritual support (especially in prayer and fasting) for my son. Early the next morning that familiar and sweet small voice awakened me with two words: "Remember Enos." It was five o'clock in the morning. With tears streaming down our cheeks Steve and I reread those first few verses of Enos. That's where Jason was even as we spoke. He had gone to hunt beasts and bugs and live off the land in the wilderness of Arizona. The possibility of complete repentance was real. He still had his agency and would choose for himself, but we believed coming soon was a chance to choose good over evil. We had *hope* in him and the faith he would choose correctly. We knelt that morning and prayed with a perfect brightness of hope. Among the words we uttered was gratitude for the scriptures and the hope contained in them.

I am learning that if we will read, even if we don't remember or understand, the Lord will use our intellects and recall to us those words in times of need. He will and does truly "speak" to us, his children, so that we will not "weary and faint" as we press forward.

Feasting upon the words of Christ also means to follow the prophets' admonitions to have regular family home evening, family prayer, and family scripture study.

When Steve and I married, we knew we were facing a huge mountain in being responsible for preparing our children for adulthood. The thoughts of helping them gain testimonies and eternal perspective was overwhelming. We decided that since we probably lacked much as teachers, the best thing, the most important thing we could do was to teach them to recognize the Holy Ghost. If they could recognize him, then not only could they gain a testimony early on but they could know when they were being inspired. The best teacher for them would be the Holy Ghost. We decided that family home evening, family prayer, and family scripture study would be the best way to invite the Spirit and point out to the children when we were feeling the Spirit.

Shortly after Steve and I were married, a General Authority visiting our stake conference read a promise from one of the prophets that "not one in a hundred" of our children would be lost if we would have family home evening. From that moment on we resolved to be consistent about our family home evening and family scripture study and family prayer. We took further hope in these efforts because of a line in Steve's blessing that says "through thy teachings thy children *will remain faithful* if thou shalt *consistently* gather them around thee and teach them with love, according to the ways of the Lord." To us this passage has meant to read and to teach from the scriptures, the Church magazines, and the words of the prophets and apostles.

Through those five dark years that Jason was lost, a brightness of hope remained because we hung on to those promises. We had been consistent. We had faith and hope in those past moments that were full of the Spirit.

I think back on the years and years of family home evenings, family prayers, family scripture studies. Most of it was not perfect, but in the moments that were, we were able to feel the Spirit, greater love was expressed, and eternal bonds were forged. That is what hope is all about.

Hope is what brought Jason back in the end. Remember what he said? He wanted to *feel* what he had *felt* when he was at *home!* He prayed for a "burning" in his heart again. The Lord gave him a physical witness as the tree burned in front of him and the spiritual witness as the Holy Ghost burned within him. He came back because there was still a spark of hope left inside of him, even if it was but an ember. He came because that spark had had its beginning in the home in family home evening, in family scripture study, and in family prayer.

Wondering how many family prayers have been offered in our home in the years Steve and I have been married, I calculated we have had approximately 10,220 family prayers to date (give or take a few hundred). That number does not include prayers in family home evening, blessings on food, prayers to open or end fasts, or other special family prayers we have had over the years.

Thinking about the accounting of our family's life on earth at the last day, it is a comfort to me to know the prayer part will be in order. I also have realized that with this amount of praying—and an equal amount of diligence—there has come great power and blessings to our family because of obedience to this counsel.

Of course, we are by no means perfect in our family prayers. I could tell you about the many times someone is out of sorts when we kneel together, or the many times we have to deal with "Hurry up, I've got things to do—let's get it over with!" Or the times we wait too long and we have to rush through the prayers before going out the door. Or the times we have held family home evening on more sincere prayers, only to hear children continue repeating their habitual, memorized sentences. Or the many times someone is asking to pray and the response is "I said it last night." There is plenty of that in our home.

The Lord hasn't asked us to be perfect in obeying the commandments. He has asked us to be perfect in striving to keep them. In other words, he has asked us to be consistent and obedient. When we started family prayer fifteen years ago, we might have had a few inspired family prayers in a year. Because of consistency over the years, not perfection, our family has been discovering that more and more often we have inspired family prayers, sometimes several in a week. We are seeing that power and blessings come from diligent family prayers.

For every commandment we obey, a blessing comes. It may not be a blessing we see immediately, but every time we obey, we are blessed. I would like to share with you what some of those blessings have been.

As we kneel, we experience the bonding that comes from praying for one another. We feel the love one for another. Often one of us will ask for a special blessing. Power and cohesiveness develop when we pray together—we feel safe with each other. The children have heard the love and concern of their parents for them. Steve and I have felt blessed and strengthened as we have heard our children pray for us. We know there is this little group of people here on earth we can always turn to and count on.

We have come to appreciate each other's individual worth. If you really want to see into someone's heart, listen to that person pray. We have listened to one another, and family prayer has helped us develop esteem for one another and for ourselves.

Family prayer has helped to diffuse contention and pride. Many times when one or more or all of us (parents included) are out of sorts or contentious, kneeling in prayer has softened those hearts and a new spirit has come forth.

Family prayer has also provided us as parents with many opportunities to teach the children how to recognize the Holy Ghost. We have been able to pause and say "Do you feel the Spirit?" "This feeling we are feeling right now is the Holy Ghost." All four of my children are able to recognize how the presence of the Holy Ghost feels, largely because of family prayer. And we have been able to invite the Holy Ghost into our home, too, through family prayer.

Through family prayer we have received counsel, comfort, understanding, answers. Often we have been able to clarify gospel principles. I remember one inspired prayer Steve offered because of our concerns about our children's choice of friends — "Help us to remember today, Father, that it is better to be alone than in the company of those who will lead us astray."

We have been able to teach gratitude and show our children that gratitude is a measuring stick of our spiritual condition. We have expressed gratitude for safety, for health, for material blessings, and for resources. Often we have had a special prayer of simply thanking Heavenly Father for answering our prayers, for things like helping our luggage to make it to our destination with us, for sparing our lives in a near head-on collision, for blessing us with resources even to go on vacation, or for blessing us to be able to get new clothes.

We have been able to teach faith and hope and strengthen that faith and hope as we have prayed together in times of need or crisis. When Chase was injured in an accident, a tender eleven-year-old Jason wept and prayed that his scars would go away. Today they are not even noticeable.

When we were trying to adopt a baby, a valiant and obedient five-year-old Chase sincerely pleaded, "Please Heavenly Father, please will you send us a baby sister, please, please, please will you?" And we were blessed with Paige.

When Steve went to take the Nevada boards, a spiritually wise and committed sixteen-year-old Ashley prayed, "Bless Dad, please. He has never given up." Steve felt good about his performance before he even knew the results.

When my father suffered a heartbreaking disappointment, a compassionate six-year-old Paige said, "Bless Papa to feel a happy spirit." My father's burden was lifted, and he felt peace again.

When a niece was in grave danger, tearful pleadings were expressed: "Help us bring her safely home." And we were able to see her rescued and brought safely home.

The night Jason called us to ask for help and to come home, he also asked the family to gather together so he could ask our forgiveness. He told the other children where he had been, what he had done, and how much he wanted to change. Tearfully he pleaded, "Will you forgive me? Will you help me? I am afraid."

Chase was the first to break the silence. With tears of love and compassion he began, "Jason, I forgive you. For six years I have prayed for you. I asked Heavenly Father to give you courage to change. I asked him to let you know how much I love you. I asked him to help you feel the Holy Ghost, and I asked him to let you know we were praying for you." Then Paige simply said, "I forgive you, too." And then Ashley expressed some deep and tender feelings to him. She concluded by saying, "It's true, Jason, what Chase said about our prayers. Hardly a day in six years has gone by that we haven't prayed for you as a family, morning and night, and also in our personal prayers. I know you came home because we have been praying for you, and if Heavenly Father can answer our prayers and send you home, he can bless you and you can change." And change he did.

Prayers are among the most powerful keys we use to unlock our eternal welfare. When it comes to prayer, there is no veil. A father shared his testimony that the prayers of the Lord's people reach heaven. His five-year-old son was hospitalized, severely ill with encephalitis while the father was away from home for several weeks to manage five businesses. The father called several times a day. He visited with his wife and family, the bishop and home teachers by phone. His grief overwhelmed him. He was desperate to be with his son and was frustrated because he could not.

He began to pray. He prayed unceasingly and without doubt. He petitioned the Lord to look after his family and if it was His will to restore his son to health. The more earnestly he prayed, the more he wanted to pray. He felt close to the Lord, to his child, to his family.

The son did recover and was released from the hospital about three weeks later. Shortly after that the father returned home. He spent time holding his son and expressing his love. Then he asked, "Stevie, what was it like being in the hospital so long? How did you feel?"

The little boy was thoughtful and then answered, "Daddy, I *heard* you."

"You heard me? What do you mean, Stevie, you *heard* me?"

"Daddy, I heard you. I heard you praying for me."

And then he repeated to this devoted father the very words he had prayed in behalf of his son. The little boy told him it helped him not to be afraid.

If we were as innocent as little Stevie, we would probably be more sensitive to those who pray for us, on both sides of the veil. Missionaries often tell of feeling their families praying for them. When members face a crisis and are humble and reaching for the Spirit, often they report of feeling lifted up by the prayers of others.

Elder John Groberg tells the story of such an experience when he was on his mission. He had been assigned to a little island somewhere in the Pacific and had to travel there by boat. A letter had been sent to the missionaries to inform them of the time of his arrival so that they could meet him at the dock. But when he arrived, no one was there to meet him. Several hours passed, the customs officer did not know what to do with Elder Groberg, and it was time to close. He decided to lock him up in the shed with other unclaimed cargo until the officer could solve the problem in the morning.

Elder Groberg looked around at his situation and began to feel alone, afraid, homesick, and hopeless. He strained to look through the cracks in the walls to catch the last rays of the sun before it set into the sea. As the sun sank, so did his spirits. He began to think of Idaho and family and home.

Suddenly he realized that it was about the exact time his family would be getting up and having breakfast. Then the miracle happened. He "heard" them praying for him, calling him by name and asking Heavenly Father to bless him on his mission. Peace filled his heart, he was comforted, and he knew he would be all right.

Whether or not we ever feel others' prayers for us or others feel ours for them, the power of prayer is not diminished. It is a great, great power in our lives and one that offers a sip from the cup of hope.

Over the years we have often wondered — *is this working?* It *is* working — in my home, in our prophet's home, in the stake president's home, in the bishop's home, in your own home. And one day, as we stand looking back on earthly family life, we will see in those many imperfect, ordinary prayers the moments of extraordinary, perfect inspiration, and we will realize how much they were binding and bonding moments and turning points for our family members — moments that helped move us along, not just in time, but for all eternity.

In the temple we learn that the true order of prayer is many. When we kneel together, we are indeed many — and strength and power are increased. I can look ahead with confidence to the trials yet to come, knowing we have this great tool, family prayer.

We have been *consistent* — not perfect — long enough now that we can see the fruits of our labors. We are witnesses for the inspired admonition to have regular family prayer, family home evening, and family scripture study. The full force of hope stems from these great tools.

Feasting upon the word of Christ becomes more fully effective when yoked with personal prayer as well. I thought I knew how to pray when all this trouble with Jason started happening. The day he left, the Spirit told me he wasn't coming back and we would not be able to teach him again in our home.

At first I prayed that his heart would be softened and he would come home. Then one day it struck me that the Lord had already told me no. Jason belonged to the Lord, not to me. So I adjusted my prayers, asking that the Lord would watch over him and inspire him to change. As I learned more about agency, my prayers changed again. My petitions included that into his life might be sent people or events that would influence him for good. And when the right moment came, would the Lord please withhold the hand of Satan long enough that Jason could contrast good over evil? Because, I told him, I believed, in the end, Jason would choose the good. My prayers were full of hope but respectful of Jason's agency.

I learned to pray that the Lord would "show me my part." No longer would my son accept my influence, and I could not choose for him, but the Lord knew what I *could* do. Would he please continue to show me my part?

Through prayers, my zealousness to have him repent and return was softened. I was tutored many times in only a sentence or two, but the words were always direct and just enough to learn truths about agency, love, patience, sorrow, joy, and hope.

When the wilderness survival program counselors called from Arizona and said, "Come pick up your boy. He is ready to come home," they told us he had had a spiritual experience but wanted to tell us himself. That is all the information we had. We flew to Phoenix and drove out to the designated rendezvous point. From there we were then driven several hours to the wilderness area. We arrived just before dark.

We had brought with us what we had been told to bring: our sleeping bags, because we were going to spend the night out there with him, and food. He had not eaten much in sixty days, only what he picked, hunted, or gathered. His request list included fried chicken and cookies, just to mention a couple of items.

As we stood under the pine trees, two counselors made a fire and explained that Jason had left his solo area early that morning. The "walk out" was extremely important as a final part of the program. He and his companion-leader, Brent, would cover thirty-five to forty miles that day over some of the roughest terrain in the Arizona wilderness. They anticipated their arrival in about two hours.

Near the end of the second hour, some doubt was expressed about whether or not Jason and Brent would make it in that night. One leader felt they would camp and come on in the morning. He explained how in some places on this particular trail they would have had to crawl on their hands and knees. He knew they hadn't eaten much the day before, either. He was sure they couldn't make it in one day.

But the seasoned leader of the group, Ezekiel, moved to the edge of the fire, stretched out to warm his hands and without looking up quietly said, "Oh, they *will* be here. Jason won't let Brent camp the night. The two most important people to him in the world, the two *who love him the most*, are here at the end of this trail. He can't wait to tell them what's happened to him. He can't wait for them to see the change. And then, there is also the food. No, he *will* be here." One hour later they arrived.

During that last hour of waiting we didn't say much to one another. Of course we were full of anticipation, our hearts pounding. But I had time to think about Ezekiel's remarks. How like this life was Jason's "walking out." We come to this wilderness of mortal life. We have to travel across some pretty rough places at times, often on spiritual hands and knees. But the valiant know that at the end are the people who love us the most—our Heavenly Parents and the Savior—and we can't wait to tell them what's happened to us. We can't wait for them to see the changes in us. We want to be able to tell them, "I have fought a good fight, I have finished my course, I have kept the faith" (2 Timothy 4:7).

And we want to hear their words of approval, "Well done." And then, there will be the *food!* The spiritual feast will continue until we grow into godhood.

We do not have to go hungry as we trek the wilderness of mortal life. We can feast upon the words of Christ and "know all things" what we must do. There are mountains we must cross. I am certain of that. But, nourished by the words of Christ, we can make it. And I know that sorrow and suffering require us to stretch beyond our grasp.

The "vast community of believers" to which we belong offers the reassurance that we are not alone in our sorrows. Others have suffered before us, others suffer with us, others will yet suffer. As we search the scriptures, feasting upon the word of Christ, we will replace faintness and weariness of mind with the knowledge that we are pursuing the will of God. We will begin to understand that, yes, the world is full of sorrow, but with a perfect brightness of hope and feasting upon the words of Christ, we will be strengthened to overcome it.

Chapter Five

A Love of God and of All Men

Hope is quickly extinguished when our thoughts focus on our own problems, frailties, weaknesses, and burdens. A man of great faith and hope, the apostle Peter, allowed himself to become distracted and lose his focus:

"And when the disciples saw him walking on the sea, they were troubled, saying, It is a spirit; and they cried out for fear.

"But straightway Jesus spake unto them, saying, Be of good cheer; it is I; be not afraid.

"And Peter answered him and said, Lord, if it be thou, bid me come unto thee on the water.

"And he said, Come. And when Peter was come down out of the ship, he walked on the water, to go to Jesus.

"But when he saw the wind boisterous, he was afraid; and beginning to sink, he cried, saying, Lord, save me.

"And immediately Jesus stretched forth his hand, and caught him, and said unto him, O thou of little faith, wherefore didst thou doubt?" (Matthew 14:26–31).

Peter was full of faith as long as he kept his focus on the Savior. "But when he saw the wind boisterous, he was afraid," and then he began to sink. We often find ourselves cast upon troubled waters in this life. As we are pitched about on the stormy seas, we can remain full of faith and hope if we keep our focus on the Savior. If we allow ourselves to become distracted by problems or adversity, or wealth, intelligence, weakness, careers, good looks, talents, and so on, we can lose our focus. Then, when the stormy seas rage, we sink into despair. It is then hard to hear above the storm the Savior's reassurance to "be of good cheer." If keeping our eyes focused on the Savior meant keeping only one commandment, what do you suppose that would be? The Savior answered that question for us:

"Master, which is the great commandment in the law? Jesus said unto him, Thou shalt love the Lord thy God with all thy heart, and with all thy soul, and with all thy mind. This is the first and great commandment. And the second is like unto it, Thou shalt love thy neighbour as thyself" (Matthew 22:36–39).

All the other laws are based on these two commandments. The law of obedience, the first law of heaven, is based on love of God: "If ye love me, keep my commandments" (John 14:15). The other laws of God are meant to teach us to sacrifice. Sacrifice teaches us to be unselfish; an unselfish heart can then be taught to love; love is what God is all about. Sacrifice teaches us how to be like God.

It has been my experience that sacrifice, eventually, is for me. Sacrifice really does bring forth the blessings of heaven. The more I give and give up, the more I get, not only in temporal blessings but even more so in spiritual ones.

The Lord does not require us to be perfect in his covenants and commandments in this life. He doesn't require that we understand them all. He doesn't even require that we agree with him. What he requires from us is that we give him our hearts—love—and are willing—desire—to be obedient.

"Behold, the Lord requireth the heart and a willing mind" (D&C 64:34).

Obedience is the key. Obedience requires sacrifice, not knowledge, understanding, agreement, or perfection. Adam didn't understand the covenants as he built an altar and offered sacrifices. The angel asked him, "Why dost thou offer sacrifices unto the Lord?" And Adam said unto him: "I know not, save the Lord commanded me." The angel did explain it all to him, but Adam had done this because the Lord "gave unto them commandments, that they should worship the Lord their God, and should offer the firstlings of their flocks, for an offering unto the Lord. And Adam was obedient unto the commandments of the Lord" (Moses 5:6, 5).

Another who didn't understand was Nephi. "Wherefore, the Lord hath commanded me to make these plates for a wise purpose in him, which purpose I know not." But he was willing to obey. "But the Lord knoweth all things from the beginning; wherefore, he prepareth a way to accomplish all his works among the children of men" (see 1 Nephi 9:5–6). Nephi worked to develop his divine potential as he sacrificed his time and energy to carefully inscribe on those plates.

We have a good friend, a dentist, who goes to Egypt every year with the Brigham Young University archaeology team. He is the forensic member of the team. His love of archaeology and the gospel prompted his curiosity about the golden plates. He had manufactured a plate of 24–karat gold that is probably very close to what Nephi used in thickness, hardness, and dimensions. Using hand-engraving tools, he tried to copy some Egyptian hieroglyphics from the Anton manuscript onto the plates, but he couldn't control the tools. After many frustrating attempts he abandoned the hand tools in favor of his high-speed dental drill. That worked much better. He copied the characters from the Anton manuscript over and over again.

He was completely astonished at how arduous a task it was. He worked for forty minutes a day every day for six months and was able to inscribe only one side plus about half the other side. It took one and a half hours to inscribe one line. He said the Nephite prophets may have been able to work a little faster with their hand tools than he had, but the high-speed dental drill probably compensated for his lack of familiarity with the method of inscribing.

He bore to us his testimony of his great respect for the Book of Mormon prophets. Theirs was not an easy task. They didn't have the high-tech tools of today. They labored and sacrificed long hours to diligently obey the Lord in recording the history and prophecies. He testified of his love for Nephi and the other prophets for working so faithfully at so difficult a task. He also said that if Church members could appreciate that labor of love firsthand, as he did, they would treasure that Book of Mormon that we print so efficiently and inexpensively today!

What a great man was Abraham, who not only didn't understand why he should sacrifice Isaac but probably didn't agree with the Lord at all. And yet, willing to be obedient, he prepared himself to sacrifice his beloved son. He was willing to give all to keep his yoke firmly fastened to the Master.

Mary was another who didn't understand as she humbly asked "How shall this be?" Then a few minutes later, her reply to the angel's explanation was a reply of obedience. "Behold the handmaid of the Lord; be it unto me according to thy word" (Luke 1:34, 38).

All through the history of this world are hundreds of examples, many recorded in the scriptures, of great men and great women who didn't understand or even agree with the commandments given unto them, but they yoked themselves to Jesus Christ by their sacrifices, their obedience. These individuals were not perfect in their mortal lives; they were men and women just like us, becoming greater still because they were trying.

"Behold, the Lord requireth the heart and a willing mind"—and then comes the promise—"and the willing and obedient shall eat the good of the land of Zion in these last days" (D&C 64:34). I believe in those words. Obedience means blessings to us, and one of those blessings is the blessing of renewed hope.

"Come unto me, all ye that labour and are heavy laden, and I will give you rest" (Matthew 11:28). The rest the Savior promises is the peace and hope we gain from knowing that because we are willing to sacrifice and obey (even if we don't always understand or agree), the Savior is on the other side pleading our case to the Father. We are with him, and he is with us. His is the sweetest peace and hope the human heart can feel.

Nephi said that in keeping a "perfect brightness of hope" we must have "a love of God and of all men." Developing that love comes from the sacrifices we make in forsaking sins, maintaining personal discipline, performing temple work, researching our genealogy, carrying out our Church callings, giving compassionate service, doing our home teaching and visiting teaching, paying our tithes and offerings, and rendering missionary service. Joseph Smith taught that "a religion that does not require the sacrifice of all things never has power sufficient to produce the faith [and hope] necessary unto life and salvation. . . . When a man has offered in sacrifice all that he has for truth's sake, not even withholding his life, and believing before God that . . . he seeks to do his will, he does know, most assuredly, that God does and will accept his sacrifice. . . . Under these circumstances, then, he can obtain the faith necessary . . . to lay hold on *eternal life"* (*Lectures on Faith,* Salt Lake City: Deseret Book Co., p. 69; italics added).

To lay hold on eternal life is the greatest hope we have. Eternal life is a life of love, a love of God and of all men. To have faith in God, we have to love him. To love him, we have to sacrifice. But in that sacrifice we learn to love others. In the end, our sacrifice is all for us. We become more and more like the Savior, who sacrificed ultimately and completely.

At Jason's missionary farewell, his thirteen-year-old brother bore a testimony of his understanding of sacrifice. He began by sharing some things from a blessing he had received. He continued:

"My blessing says I will have many learning and growing experiences and I will draw upon them from my family. It says I will then be able to share these understandings of the Lord's plan to others. I will be able to tell of the great importance of a good family and assure them this is the Lord's plan; that the family is eternal and the greatest blessings can be obtained with the experiences you share with your family. I have come to understand that the experiences that my blessing talks about are not always happy ones.

"The experience that we had with Jason hurt a lot, but I learned how to love more and to sacrifice. Those years that Jason was gone I never gave up. My faith grew stronger and stronger. I prayed that Heavenly Father would give him the courage to change and to think of his family and to know that we were praying for him. The strength from my family helped me believe that the Lord would answer my prayers.

"The night he came home, I knew my prayers and my family's prayers had been answered, because he told us that he was thinking and feeling us pray for him and he knew we could help him. . . .

"After he left for the wilderness, the family decided we

would fast every Sunday until he came home. We fasted ten Sundays in a row. Through this unhappy experience I gained a good experience through the sacrifice of all that food. It made me love Jason even more and feel even closer to him. I knew the Lord could accept my sacrifice and bless him to change. He did!"

Sacrifice of love, prayer, fasts, and service to others helped us as a family to love Jason more during his years of absence, not less. Not a day in five years went by that prayers were not offered. Sometimes we worried that our children would grow discouraged and lose hope. Chase's testimony at the farewell bore a powerful witness that sacrifice does work. It works not only for those we sacrifice for but also for ourselves.

After Jason left for the survival course, we decided as a family to fast every Sunday until he came home. Everyone was eager except eight-year-old Paige. She thought it was a horrible idea. The two older ones got after her, saying her brother needed her more than she needed the food. Reluctantly, she agreed.

We were all touched when she came to the car after church that first Sunday, carefully protecting a giant cookie that had been given out in Primary. She explained to us how much she wanted to eat it, but she knew her brother needed her more.

We all learned through this experience that if we will give the best offering we can, sparing nothing, we can lay those offerings on the altar and tell Heavenly Father, This is the best we can do. We can with truth tell him we have given the most, in money, time, love, prayers, fasts, and so forth, that we possibly could. Then we can with confidence ask him to accept the offering and please bless our loved one, or our efforts.

During this time we wrote Jason and told him these things. Then we told him that he could participate with us. If he would sacrifice his sins and kneel down and repent, then the Savior would stand before the Father in behalf of him. The Savior could say, "I gave all I had, even my life. Please forgive Jason."

Sacrifice brings forth the blessing of heaven.

When we are heavy burdened with piloting our vessels in stormy seas, we don't feel like going visiting teaching or home teaching. Especially during a crisis it's hard to get up, get dressed, and fulfill a Church calling. But during those times we feel like doing it the least, we need to do it the most.

The first reason is obvious. It takes our minds off our problems. Self-centeredness turns into selflessness. Often we find a lift and peace as we give to others. We come home comforted.

The second reason is called the Law of the Harvest. We reap what we sow. If we plant fear and hopelessness, we get back bushels of it. If we plant love and hope, we are filled with gifts. If we take care of the Lord first and put his work above our own demands, then in times of need we can with confidence ask him to help us.

When our loved ones reject our love and help, if we serve diligently to help others, our sacrifices will be sanctified. There will come into the lives of our loved ones those who will water the seeds we have planted.

In a talk entitled "The Spark of Faith," Bishop Henry B. Eyring quoted President J. Reuben Clark, Jr.:

" 'It is my hope and my belief that the Lord never permits the light of faith wholly to be extinguished in any human heart, however faint the light may glow. The Lord has provided that there shall still be there a spark which, with teaching, with the spirit of righteousness, with love, with tenderness, with example, with living the gospel, shall brighten and glow again, however darkened the mind may have been. And if we shall fail so to reach those among us of our own whose faith has dwindled low, we shall fail in one of the main things which the Lord expects at our hands' (in Conference Report, Oct. 1936, p. 114)" (in Conference Report, Nov. 1986, p. 74).

We hold a lot of meetings in our church that are inspiring and motivating. We talk a lot about doing more. But are we just "talking the talk"? Too often, talking becomes a substitute for doing. Whenever we multiply by zero, the answer is always zero. One million times zero sounds like a lot, but it is still only zero. We have to put our efforts where our talk is. It is only in the "doing" that hope becomes a reality in loving God and others.

Members of the Church around the world remember President Spencer W. Kimball's motto, Do It. That expression was a household phrase while he was our prophet. We had hope in those words because his example in "doing" made it believable. A few years before he died I was told the following story by the Relief Society president of the stake where President Kimball lived in Salt Lake City:

"It seems that a young man moved into one of the basement apartments with his girlfriend. This was at a time when this liberal behavior was just beginning to shake the roots of conservative Salt Lake City. This young man was the son of a prominent Church member. The ward was appalled and shocked at his arrogant behavior. Evidently the gossip and disapproval were running profusely.

"Then one Sunday he appeared at church. He returned again and again. Soon the girlfriend moved out. As time passed he participated in all the ordinances of the gospel. The reason for his change of heart was soon discovered.

"One Sunday afternoon he said he was watching football on television. His girlfriend was taking a nap. The doorbell rang, and he got up to open it. There standing on his porch were President and Sister Kimball with a loaf of homemade bread. The prophet extended his hand in friendship and said

'Hello, I am Brother Kimball. This is my wife, Sister Kimball, and we are here to welcome you into the ward.'

"This young man was touched and shaken by the love of President and Sister Kimball. It was irresistible to him that one so great would reach out in care and concern for him. It changed his life."

Where did President Kimball learn to love and care so much? He learned it from one greater than himself, who "so loved the world he sent His only begotten son" That same Only Begotten Son who loved us so much that he came "into the world that he may save all men if they will hearken unto his voice; for behold, he suffereth the pains of all men, yea, the pains of every living creature, both men, women, and children, who belong to the family of Adam" (2 Nephi 9:21).

We have a solemn obligation to reach past our own grief into the hearts of those who need us and will accept our help. When we do so and keep sacred the trust that God "expects at our hands," then someone will do the same for our own wayward loved ones.

During some of the darkest days, I still had to serve in some capacity or another. Looking back, I see how great a blessing it was. Through my service, peace and hope continued to grow in my heart because service gave me a better focus. There were days that I just didn't want to go do the work. But afterwards, the strength and love from others always was a great comfort. The greatest comfort also came from the most private and personal service.

My special mission is mostly the unseen, unsung acts of service, and most of that is within the walls of my own home.

The people who have influenced me the most are those who have touched my life one-to-one. They have been the ones who gave me hope, who showed me hope by their teachings, their examples, or their love for me. I think back on the sacrifices of my parents, my Primary and Sunday School teachers, my Young Women leaders, Relief Society presidents, bishops and stake presidents, home teachers and visiting teachers. Their love for me has given me a lifetime of hope. Certainly those people who have served me must have also felt my love for them. Through sacrifice we gain hope with a "love of God and of all men."

In a Primary class I received my testimony that this is the true church of God. Our class was being prepared for baptism by a faithful Primary teacher. I cannot remember what she looked like, I don't remember her name, but I will never forget her spirit and her testimony.

One afternoon when we met on the stage in the cultural hall for class, the discussion was about Joseph Smith and the Book of Mormon. I do not remember one word of what she said, but I'll never forget how I felt. Her testimony was full of love, encouragement, and truth. The desire to know for myself just welled up inside of me. I mentally faded out of the class and thought, How can I know, really know, this is true?

What happened next is the first experience that I can actually remember as something spiritually significant in my life. The sweetest, warmest feeling filled me as a voice spoke to my heart: "This is my church, Anita, and Joseph Smith was a true prophet of God."

My seven-year-old mind could not comprehend what had happened, but my heart did. Somehow, I knew the Church was true. As I have pondered that moment over the years, I have appreciated the great woman who was my Primary teacher. Her testimony captured my attention. The Spirit filled the room. She loved me, and I knew that. She was an important part of my wanting that knowledge for myself. Her love was a point of hope.

She doesn't know what she has done for me. She has no

idea what special mission she had in my life, and won't, until the next life when I can tell her. I've wondered, does she ever feel hopeless? I wonder if she could ever know how much hope she helped me gain.

There was a Young Women advisor who doesn't know of her significance in my life, either. One day she appeared at my door with a red rose, and with tears in her eyes she told me how much she loved me. She had been thinking about me that day, she said, and brought me this rose to show me that one day I would be in full blossom and just as beautiful. She assured me that she saw in me a great woman.

How could she have known that I was about to walk out the door and into a terrible mistake? She doesn't have any idea what she has done for me. I don't even remember her name, but she touched my life, forever.

Another advisor in charge of a ward talent show when I was young must have noticed me sitting out all the talent nights. She came to me and said she had a poem she wanted me to memorize for the talent show. It seemed to me in my rebellious mind that she was just condescending to me. She was just giving me something to do because she was obligated to include everyone. But she showed love toward me and helped me by teaching me how to make this poem "alive" just with my expressions. Little does she know she introduced me to a talent I didn't know I had. Every time someone remarks about my ability to express myself, I think of her, the love she gave me, and the hope she instilled in my heart.

Laurie was a beautiful teenager, homecoming-queen beautiful. She had a flawless complexion, long silken blonde hair, radiant eyes, and a delightful personality to match. Wherever she went heads would turn as people stretched their necks to glimpse her beauty.

One Sunday she appeared at church with a new friend. He

was unshaven, with a full beard and long hair. He wore jeans and bikers boots and a leather vest studded with metal emblems. Instead of a watch he wore leather wrist straps (no one would have believed he could tell time anyway). The ward was in shock. What was this magnificent young woman doing with this misfit? Her family must have been upset and worried.

He continued to attend church with her and began taking the missionary discussions. He accepted the challenge to be baptized, and the date was set. When he arrived at the chapel that baptismal day, he was unrecognizable. He had cut his hair and shaved his face and was wearing a suit and tie. Underneath that facade had been an absolutely breathtakingly handsome young man! No one could have believed how *good*-looking he really was. But Laurie had seen it.

He continued to grow in the gospel and his testimony, and one day he announced he had decided to go on a mission. As he stood to say farewell to the ward, he gave credit for his new life to the Savior and to Laurie. They had seen in him something he had not even seen in himself. The "love of God and of all men" brings hope, an abundance of hope.

A good friend was given a new visiting teaching assignment. She was told, "Good luck. This woman hates the sisters at church." My friend mentioned her assignment to others, who also responded with the same sentiment. My friend scheduled the first visit and arrived on time. The door was opened by an overweight, unhappy-looking woman. My friend sensed a spirit of great depression as she entered the dimly lighted home. My friend sat close to this sister and during the course of the visit, casually took her hand and held it for a long time.

This small act of love softened the woman, and she began to share her guilt about being inactive in the Church. She wept about her efforts to lose weight. She opened up to my friend as she had never done to anyone before. The visiting teacher promised to help. She would walk with her for one hour three times a week. She would bring her special recipes. She would be available as a "hotline" during moments of temptation.

One hour later the visiting teacher who had arrived as a stranger left as a friend. Standing on the doorstep, the woman threw her arms around my friend and said, "I needed someone like you. I felt so hopeless." The small expression of love in taking her hand renewed hope. Today this sister is active in Church and feeling good about herself again.

A husband and wife I'll call Jim and Martha brought hope back into their lives as they brought hope to someone else through love and service. They had been married thirty years. Their children were doing well, their financial security was established, they were enjoying life and each other, they were the best of friends. Then the devastating news came that Martha was dying. It was a slow-growing disease but an incurable one. She could expect to live two, maybe three more years. After the anger, denial, and sorrow of it all passed, they began to make plans. They would travel and visit their children and spend all their time together.

Then at a Church auxiliary meeting it came to Martha's attention that a family in their ward was in need. The husband was not active in the Church; the wife, who was not a member, had recently had a stroke and was paralyzed permanently. She was only twenty-nine years old and the couple had three small children. Their meager savings were gone, spent on hospital bills. The husband was struggling to look after the children, maintain a job, and care for his invalid wife.

Martha went home from that meeting touched deeply by the plight of these people. For the first time since hearing of her own condition, she felt the relief of being concerned for someone else. Through a sleepless night she thought about how good her life with Jim had been, how blessed and full.

This illness was a mountain for them, but they had the hope of eternal life together someday. She knew they had the resources to alleviate some suffering for this young couple. What would the Savior do? For the first time in months she felt a brightness of hope. "This is right," she thought. She felt the Spirit moving her towards a love of God and of all men.

When morning came she told Jim of her restless night, of her promptings to help, of the hope she was feeling. She said that to travel would be nice, but after she was gone Jim would only have photographs and a few memories of that time. If they helped this family, Jim would see the fruits of their labors for years to come. She asked him if that wasn't what the gospel was all about? She could die having been productive to the end, and she said it would bring peace to everyone.

Jim could not disagree. He felt the Spirit, and he sensed renewed hope. That morning they knelt in prayer for guidance, for inspiration, for love. That evening they paid their first visit to this needy little family.

In the two years and eight months that followed they brought hope into the lives of this couple. They remodeled their living room, adding a bigger window so the mother could watch her children at play and be able to enjoy the outside. Jim and Martha bought her a special bed so she could be more comfortable by her window to the world. They worked hard planting a rose garden right in front of this window, and they also maintained the yard work. They spent countless hours tending the children and holding them, trying to comfort them as their mother no longer could. They took the children on short trips with them, to the park, on numerous picnics. They made sure they went to church every Sunday. Jim and Martha made special meals twice a week and had family home evening Monday with the family. It wasn't long before the father was attending church again. And soon after that his wife wanted the missionary lessons.

The stake missionaries were called in, and Jim and Martha helped make every meeting a special event. It was a joyous and emotional day when Jim helped lower this young wife and mother into the baptismal font. Tears streamed down his cheeks as he helped support her fragile body while her husband raised his hand to the square and began, "Having been commissioned of Jesus Christ . . . "

That night Martha told Jim, "These have been the best years of my life. I love the Lord, I love life, I am at peace."

Martha was too ill to attend the temple to see them sealed. But Jim reported back every detail, and when the photographs arrived she lovingly memorized each one. Martha passed away several months later.

The fast Sunday after the funeral, the young husband bore his testimony of the Savior's love in his life. He said he had seen the Savior on the faces of Jim and Martha. Love, he said, had brought back hope into his life and the lives of his family. Even the hope, he wept, of eternal life.

Not long after that his wife also died. The hours before her passing were peaceful ones. As the family and loved ones gathered around her, she whispered with subdued excitement, "Oh, it's so beautiful! It's so beautiful! I see my grandfather; he's there! And Martha—I see Martha! She is so happy!"

A love of God and of all men brings a true and perfect brightness of hope, even to the end.

We would all love to be good Samaritans, perhaps even in the same way Jim and Martha were, but the cost today to do what the good Samaritan did would probably be somewhere between ten and fifteen thousand dollars. Through the combined funds of fast offerings, however, we can all share in being good Samaritans. The fast offerings are special funds.

Likewise, in a world of little love, where people's hearts have "waxed cold," generally speaking, it may be impossible for one person to make much of a difference. But through the combined efforts of Church callings and missionary work, home teaching and visiting teaching, we can work together to change the world enough to prepare it for the Second Coming. We can all share in this great love and it is special love.

When we took Jason to the Missionary Training Center, we met a woman who was taking a homemade treat to a missionary already there. She lived about one hundred miles away and had driven to Provo to leave this young man some fresh, home-made cookies and brownies. Was he her son? No, he was the son of the missionary who had baptized her almost thirty years earlier! That missionary had served and loved and taught her the gospel through his sacrifice as a missionary. He served and loved and taught his own son the gospel through his sacrifices as a parent. Now this sister in the gospel could serve the son through her love and sacrifice. The young missionary some-where in that Missionary Training Center would carry on the momentum. Hope is passed on through love and service from generation to generation.

One of the places that has always brought hope to me, especially in the years Jason was gone, is the temple. Here Church members have the unique opportunity to sacrifice in giving service to those who cannot help themselves. The work performed in the temple does bring a love of God and of all men. It brings *hope*. Attending the temple always leaves me with the feeling that we really do have a chance to make it to the celestial kingdom.

Elder Vaughn J. Featherstone, president of the Utah South Area of the Church, spoke these words at the Manti Temple in April of 1987.

"Before the Savior comes the world will darken. There

will come a period of time where even the elect will lose hope if they do not come to the temples. The world will be so filled with evil that the righteous will only feel secure within these walls. The Saints will come here not only to do vicarious work, but to find a haven of peace. They will long to bring their children here for safety's sake. . . .

"We will not be alone in our temples. . . .

"The covenants and ordinances will fill us with faith as a living fire. In a day of desolating sickness, scorched earth, barren wastes, sickening plagues, disease, destruction, and death, we as a people will rest in the shade of trees, we will drink from the cooling fountains. We will abide in places of refuge from the storm; we will mount up as on eagles' wings; we will be lifted out of an insane and evil world. We will be as fair as the sun and clear as the moon.

"When the Savior comes he will honor His people. Those who are spared and prepared will be a temple-loving people. They will know Him.

"Our children will bow down at His feet and worship Him as the Lord of Lords, the King of Kings. They will bathe His feet with their tears and He will weep, and bless them for having suffered through the greatest trials known to man.

"Let us prepare them with the faith to surmount every trial and every condition. We will do it in these holy, sacred temples."

Even though several weeks had passed after Jason left, my grief was not diminishing. It occurred to me that the temple would be the place to find some relief from the suffering, as well as some answers. The session was peaceful, but the heart-healing comfort never came. As I sat through the closing moments of the session, listening to the final words, suddenly it was as a brilliant light filled the room — a perfect light, a perfect brightness of hope. Within those words was a witness of what the temple means to families. Tears of joy and awe streamed down my face as understanding came to me about how the temple endowment is a huge priesthood umbrella that protects us and our posterity. If we will obey and live the covenants we make there, somehow all our posterity will be better off because of our obedience, not just in this life but in the one to come as well. Now my prayers had new meaning. But the principle took on a new dimension. I had powers to bless my child's life, powers of hope, if I would live up to my temple covenants. It was a moment of great hope, and my tormented heart was peaceful. The temple endowment and sealings are keys of power to us and to our families. Attending the temple often renews our faith and hope in those sealings.

The temples that dot the earth today are witnesses of faith, hope, and charity. Entering the temple is like opening the gate to eternity. For a short time, within those walls, we are in the foyer of our celestial home. What hope awaits us on that threshold!

The influence of the temple can also strengthen us outside its walls. When Jason's wilderness leaders called to say they were giving him only one more week, we called our extended family together. We asked them to join in fasting and praying with us for him. Several days later, before dawn, came another prompting. "Jason needs many prayers today." Immediately I thought of all the people who were praying for him and that should be enough. Then again, "Jason needs many prayers today." I began to think of six or seven good friends we could call upon when again the impression said, "Jason needs MANY prayers today." This time the word *many* was emphasized. "Many," I thought. "*Many* prayers. The true order of prayer is *many*. Where did I learn that? In the temple!"

During the next hour I called every temple in the United States and had Jason's name put on the temple prayer rolls.

That day, literally, thousands were praying for him! Later we learned that that was the day he had the spiritual experience that changed his life. It was another testimony to me of the power of the temple in our lives, not only as individuals, but as eternal families as well. When a couple kneels at the altar it isn't so much so that they can live together forever as it is that they will receive the patriarchal keys and powers that will enable them to get to that kingdom where they can live together forever. The temple has increased my love for the Lord and for others, and it has strengthened my hope.

A love of God and of all men also strengthens our self-esteem. That self-esteem is needed to combat Satan's taunting slings and arrows as he tries to show us our weaknesses. Unlike the inspiration to improve that comes when the Lord reveals to us our weaknesses, Satan's words are always full of hopelessness.

Through our obedience and sacrifices we grow "to love God and all men," and thus have greater self-esteem and feelings of self-worth. Ammon tried to explain that to his brothers, but they misunderstood. Sometimes so do we.

"My brothers and my brethren, behold I say unto you, how great reason have we to rejoice; for could we have supposed when we started from the land of Zarahemla that God would have granted unto us such great blessings? And now, I ask, what great blessings has he bestowed upon us? Can ye tell? Behold, I answer for you; for our brethren, the Lamanites, were in darkness, yea, even in the darkest abyss, but behold, how many of them are brought to behold the marvelous light of God! And this is the blessing which hath been bestowed upon us, that we have been made instruments in the hands of God to bring about this great work. Behold, thousands of them do rejoice, and have been brought into the fold of God. . . .

"For if we had not come up out of the land of Zarahemla,

these our dearly beloved brethren, who have so dearly beloved us, would still have been racked with hatred against us, yea, and they would also have been strangers to God" (Alma 26:1–4, 9).

It seemed to his brothers that Ammon was bragging about what great work they had accomplished:

"His brother Aaron rebuked him, saying: Ammon, I fear that thy joy doth carry thee away unto boasting" (Alma 26:10).

But Ammon understood that when we are obedient and are willing to sacrifice all things, we feel a deep love for God and for our fellowman, and we feel strength and are full of hope. That is true self-esteem.

"But Ammon said unto him: I do not boast in my own strength, nor in my own wisdom; but behold, my joy is full, yea, my heart is brim with joy, and I will rejoice in my God. Yea, I know that I am nothing; as to my strength I am weak; therefore I will not boast of myself, but I will boast of my God, for in his strength I can do all things; yea, behold, many mighty miracles we have wrought in this land, for which we will praise his name forever" (Alma 26:11–12).

Ammon was humble but full of strength, a strength not of his own but from his realization that the Lord was blessing him with strength. What love for God he must have felt! What love for the people! What strength and hope he personally felt! Is that not the great spirit our missionaries carry with them? They are special messengers of *hope,* teaching the words of eternal life to all the ends of the earth.

In loving God and others, we have to be sincere. The word *sincere* has an interesting origin. It is from two Latin words, *sine,* which means "without" and *cera,* which means "wax."

In ancient Rome wealthy families commissioned sculptors to make busts of themselves to be placed in their homes — like having portraits painted today.

The ancient Roman home was built around an atrium. Most of the rooms opened to this central area, which was exposed to the sun and elements. The busts would be placed on pedestals and displayed in the atrium.

As Rome became prosperous and wealthier, the demand for the busts increased. The sculptors could not keep up with the demand. Many began using inferior grades of marble, which was softer and easier to work with than the higher quality grades. It had cracks in it or developed them as sculptors worked with it. To hide the flawed stone, artists filled the cracks with wax and polished the patches until they took on the appearance of fine marble.

But because the sculpture was displayed in sunny atriums, the wax soon melted and the flawed marble was exposed. The inferior workmanship began to affect even the quality craftsmen. Soon sculptors who valued their reputation and insisted only on producing quality art began to advertise and guarantee their work as *sinecera* — "without wax."

Sincere means pure, original, genuine, without hypocrisy or pretending, without falsehood. *Sincere* has come to mean that we have hearts that are true and genuine. The wax that we use to cover our sins and gratify ourselves is pride. When our hearts are cracked with hopelessness or fear, if we don't humble ourselves to allow the Savior to heal our hearts, we are in danger of reaching for the wax of pride.

Anne Morrow Lindbergh once said, "The most exhausting work in life is insincerity" (*Gift from the Sea*, Pantheon, 1977, p. 12).

I know what she meant. The first thirty or so years of my life I was nearly worn out from being insincere. When we try to paint to others our seemingly perfect life, or when we refuse to let the Lord reveal our weaknesses to ourselves, we become exhausted keeping ourselves from being exposed.

That is not to say we should drag our problems like baskets of dirty laundry from door to door wanting others to agree with us. Rather, I'm talking about revealing our true *feelings*. For example, when the wife of a stake president told the congregation in stake conference that sometimes she felt like her prayers hit the ceiling and bounced back, you could almost hear an audible gasp. She told me later she was staggered by the calls and letters she received saying, "I have felt that way, too." They expressed relief at hearing someone they admired so much be so sincere. Many told her it gave them hope.

Several things began to change when I began to reveal my feelings to others. First, I discovered others felt as I did, and a spirit-to-spirit bonding began. Second, the more open we become with one another, the more we are able to help each other, with *real* help, with our burdens. Third, the more spirit-to-spirit help we give, the more love develops and the less judgmental we become.

Often we are afraid to let others see our weaknesses because we are afraid others won't love us. My experience has shown me that others have loved me more because they feel "safe" with me. Also, recognizing and verbalizing my weaknesses has given me increased strength to work hard in trying to overcome them.

If it's too painful at first to be sincere (without the wax of pride) in front of others, we can start by being sincere in front of the Lord. With real sincerity we can ask, "Heavenly Father, will you show me *my* part?"

There is such freedom in being sincere. Sincerity not only allows us to move about in this world unfettered by behavior that always needs attention but it allows us to feel the love of God and of all men.

Our world has "waxed cold" in the love for God, for others, and for self (Matthew 24:12; D&C 45:27). Hopelessness breeds

because of selfishness, pride, apathy, insincerity, and disobedience. Pain, labor, and sacrifice have become unacceptable
in today's world. All around us we hear news of plagues, pes-
tilence, disease, war, rumors of war, earthquakes, floods, famine,
murder, adultery, divorce, terrorism, drugs, and other calam-
ities of all kinds. The hopelessness crushes in upon this world
darkened by Satan's influences.

But ever constant, growing ever brighter, and brighter yet
to be, is the hope of eternal life. That hope is like a lamp that
lights the way. That hope is very much alive. It is alive in you.
It is alive in your knowledge and testimony of the plan of
salvation and eternal life. It is alive in your love.

I think of the elders recently slain in their fields of labor.
When they stood at their farewells, they had no idea they would
not be coming home. If they had known on the day of their
farewell that they would be killed, martyred for the kingdom,
do you think they still would have gone? I believe they would
have gone, no matter what. Such is the sacrifice of one who
has a brightness of hope and a love of God and of all men.

You've been with the apostle Peter more than once in that
storm-tossed boat. Just when you think you have enough faith,
along come more waves of adversity, and you've felt that sinking
feeling, too. Just because you have a few setbacks doesn't mean
you aren't doing a good job.

The love of the Latter-day Saints for God, for each other,
and for themselves started out in 1830 as a small candle burning
brightly. Today it is a splendid torch that radiates a perfect
brightness of hope. Tomorrow it will be the only lighthouse
left that casts those rays of hope across a stormy sea. With
obedience, sacrifice, and sincerity, we will be able to look into
those beams of love and see the Savior standing upon troubled
waters. And then, illuminated with this great love, we will hear
the Master say above the boisterous wind, "Be not afraid. It is
I. Be of good cheer."

Chapter Six

Endure to the End, and Ye Shall Have Eternal Life

In my twenty-year career as a professional interior designer I have trained myself to picture things "finished." Only in recent years has it occurred to me just what it could mean in terms of spiritual direction. The word *perfect* in Latin means "finished"! It is humbling to think that from temporal work an *eternal perspective* could develop.

Developing the talent of picturing things finished — "perfect" — has come from years and years of exercising the principles of interior design, art, and architecture. I have learned to work with blueprints, drawings, and architectural specifications. There has been much practical application, trial and error, and of course, seeing jobs completed. I have had to pay close attention to detail even before there is a structure. I have had to train myself to picture the construction itself finished — I have to be able to see walls that don't yet exist. My work on a recently completed multimillion-dollar design project was begun two years before a shovel of earth was moved.

Developing eternal perspective, hope in eternal life, is very much like this training. There are plans and blueprints in the scriptures and in the counsel of the prophets. There is the practice of those principles and doctrine, for which obedience is the key. Then there is the trial and error that comes as we remove pride from our lives. And, of course, there is seeing our life's work through to the end. We have to train ourselves to picture the man or woman in Christ who does not yet exist. Hope in eternal life is the expectation and assurance that the man or woman in Christ we want to be will one day become a reality.

To be perfect is to be finished, complete, possessing all attributes of God. Picturing ourselves perfect, finished, dwelling with our Heavenly Parents is to have eternal perspective. Picturing ourselves already there is to have the ability to look past our circumstances and sorrows in this life and "on, on to the victory!" It is to be able to realize and emphasize to ourselves that these "afflictions shall be but a small moment" and if we endure them well, "God shall exalt [us] on high" (D&C 121:7, 8). To endure to the end is to have hope in the greatest goal of all, eternal life.

But that word *perfect* gets us every time. How could such a small word be used like such a big stick to beat up so many? How can that one small word cause so much hopelessness, when actually it was meant to do the opposite? It is a lot easier to think about a brightness of hope than a *perfect* brightness of hope. That one little word makes it seem an impossible goal.

The Savior said, "Be ye therefore perfect, even as your Father which is in heaven is perfect" (Matthew 5:48) because he knew we could do it. The confidence he has in us was meant to inspire us, to give us hope, not cause us to despair. He was the only perfect man to live on earth. Did he invite us to perfection just to mock us? Of course not. His invitation was meant to inspire us. It was meant to help us gain that hope in ourselves. If the Savior said, "Come, follow me," and then suffered and died, it was only because he believed many would follow him all the way to perfection.

Perfect means "finished." We are probably too often put off by that word because we refuse to appreciate the time it takes to really finish something of great quality. It takes twelve years to be formally educated. It takes four more years to gain a college degree. It takes at least half a year to build a house. It took forty years to build the Salt Lake Temple. Mary Lou Retton spent more than half her life preparing for the Olympic event in which she scored the first perfect ten ever scored in that event. How long does it take a piece of coal to become a diamond? How long does it take a struggling music student to become accomplished enough to perform in a great orchestra? How long do you think it takes to become "perfect, even as your Father in heaven"? Do we think we could possibly have all the experiences or enough of them in this lifetime to make us noble enough? I think not, our progression goes on with us into eternity until in the due time of the Lord we are "finished."

To have a "perfect" brightness of hope has nothing to do with our personal perfection but much more to do with our personal determination. It is possible to have a perfect brightness of hope without being perfect. That brightness comes "line upon line, precept upon precept; here a little, and there a little; giving us consolation by holding forth that which is to come, confirming our hope" (D&C 128:21).

"Here a little, and there a little," line by line, principle by principle, spiritual experience by spiritual experience—that's how it's been for me in my life. And if your life has been like mine, then that's how it has been for you, too. A perfect brightness of hope helps us to appreciate the little-by-little progress we are making.

Several years ago I boarded a very crowded airplane headed home from a women's conference where I had been the keynote speaker. Every seat was taken except the one next to me in the middle. The last person to get on the plane was an elderly, hard-looking woman with an angry spirit and very loud voice. That was her seat.

From the moment she seated herself, I could smell the alcohol. She began to shout at the flight attendant for a drink. She stood waving her dollar and screaming for more liquor. The flight attendant told her to sit down and put on her seat belt. She cautioned the woman about her boisterous and angry attitude. She could see that this woman had already had too much to drink.

As the passenger settled in next to me, she began to curse, taking God's name in vain. She cursed him, the pilot, the plane, the whole human race. She belched and guffawed and made all sorts of noises. I was revolted.

Then she grabbed my arm and began to cry. She was on her way to bury her brother, the last living relative she had. She didn't bother to wipe her nose. She went on about how she had buried her husband a year ago and her daughter last spring. She snorted and belched "booze" breath and continued to carry on. I was sick to my stomach.

Sitting there, with her hanging on to me, I thought of the conference I just had attended. The sweet and wholesome faces of the sisters flashed before me. Then I thought of the Savior. What would he do if he were *here?* I tried to ignore the thought, but it only grew louder and louder in my head.

For the next hour I was in turmoil. Who do you think you are, Anita Canfield? You just left a conference where you professed love and charity to five hundred women, and look at you! You cannot even be charitable to this poor disgusting creature. I was ashamed. And yet my pride stood in my way. My revulsion took over. I turned away from her and stared out the window.

I was never so glad for a trip to end. The ordeal was over, and yet, for three days she lingered in my thoughts. My pride and lack of charity kept surfacing and I kept pushing them aside until finally I felt the need to "unburden" my guilt. Acknowledging my wrong attitude and behavior, I admitted that I was not sure whether or not, if faced with the same situation, I would respond any differently. The Holy Ghost was there to inspire me. Suddenly I realized, and repeated, that at least I was making *some* progress because there once had been a day when I would have walked off that plane and never given it another thought. At least I felt recognition and remorse. I would keep trying to improve.

Before we moved from California back to Nevada, my ward sisters asked me to be their keynote speaker at the annual ward women's conference. It was very touching to be chosen from among them to teach. I prepared diligently and received some special insights given during my preparation. But nothing prepared me for what happened at the conference that morning.

These sisters, all eighty-four of them, came with the purest of hearts, full of love. They came to be taught by "one of their own." They came with complete humility. Sometimes being taught by someone you know well is a stumbling block because you know all that person's faults. These women looked past the faults they saw in me and they loved me and loved each other during those moments we shared. The Spirit healed wounds, friendships were renewed, hard feelings were put away, and two sisters were reactivated because of the spirit there that day.

I rode home from the conference in silence. The love was

almost too much to bear. That night I was in the kitchen preparing for Sunday when Steve walked in and said, "I can really feel the Spirit, Anita. You are almost glowing! It's overpowering. I don't even dare to touch you!"

With tears streaming down my cheeks I said, "I know it! This is the *best* I can be in mortal life! I can't get any better. My heart is so swollen with love that it almost hurts. I could go out in the street and bring home a bum and care for him. This is as good as I can be. Oh, Steve, I wish I could stay like this for the rest of my life. But tomorrow is Sunday, and you know what Sunday is like. And then Monday will bring the laundry, the business, the homework and Little League, and who knows what else. Before this time next week, it will all be gone, and I will be back to the real Anita!"

Slowly he walked across the kitchen, wrapped his arms around me, and said with conviction, "No! *This* is the real Anita!"

I have probably repeated this motto many times: "Be the best you can be." I don't believe it anymore. I am rarely my best, rarely like I was that moment in the kitchen. Now I believe we have to DO the best we can. If we are "pressing forward" and doing all we can, every now and then we are able to brush up against the real us and touch eternity and eternal life. Eternal life is a life of love. It comes to us "line upon line."

You know those feelings — when your heart is full, brimful of love, and you feel "a love of God and of all men." That is eternal perspective. Perhaps it doesn't come often, or at least not as often as we want it. But the desire to feel like that again keeps us enduring to the end. That is what hope is all about. That moment in my kitchen was a "perfect brightness" of hope and the thought of it helps get me through some of the darker days.

That is what a "spirit of truth" is all about. The Holy Ghost is the bearer of truth, "for the Spirit speaketh the truth and lieth not" and will show you "things as they really are" and "as they really will be" (Jacob 4:13). He can even help us see ourselves as we really will be. The gift of the Holy Ghost is such a tremendous gift. The Savior said he wouldn't leave us alone, that he would "give you another Comforter, that he may abide with you for ever; Even the Spirit of truth...for he dwelleth with you, and shall be in you. I will not leave you comfortless" (John 14:16–18).

There is a price to pay to become familiar with the language of the Holy Ghost. When we lie in bed, filled with self-pity, with our sheets pulled over our heads, we aren't paying that price. We have to *do* what the Savior said to the apostles when they were afraid in that boat on a stormy sea. He told them to "be of good cheer."

So how do we feel of good cheer? How do we hear the Holy Ghost when the pain makes the tears flow freely?

Of all the concepts of the gospel, recognizing the Spirit may be one of the most difficult to understand. The Savior called the Holy Ghost "another Comforter." The Savior could not remain on the earth to comfort us personally so he gave us the gift of the Holy Ghost, a personage of spirit to abide with us in his place.

That still, small *voice,* as he is so often called, is just that. *Still* means quiet, peaceful, bringing peace to your thoughts, order to your mind. *Small* means tiny, little, diminutive, so much so that only you can hear it. *Voice* means words, very often sounding much like our own thoughts.

The Comforter is described not only as a voice but also as a feeling. Burning, swelling, calmness, warm, comfort, assurance—these are all words we've heard used to describe the feelings the Spirit brings. There could be some confusion in trying to squeeze all those descriptions into an explanation of how he feels. At times we need to "burn" in our hearts, as we do when we ask if the Church is true. At times we feel "warm," as when we listen to an inspired talk. At times we feel calm, as in the face of danger. Probably all these assorted descriptions really do *feel* very much alike. Depending on our personality and emotions, we find different ways to express the feeling. The most important part is that we are able to recognize the Spirit when we feel it.

When the president of a huge southern California stake Relief Society picked me up at the airport, she cautioned me to be prepared for a very poor turnout that night. She related all the troubles their stake had been experiencing. There had been unusual growth, wards had been divided, people were feeling left out—in one ward members were suing each other and there had been many excommunications. I felt like turning back right then!

She was right. Very few women showed up. I knew the attendance indicated that it was going to be a long hour at the pulpit. It was.

For a little over an hour I struggled for the Spirit. The congregation was not with me. The feeling in the room was flat. Apathy was so thick I could taste it. I wanted my talk to be over.

Then something changed during the last twenty minutes. I felt the women's hearts open up to the words and *feelings* of the message. We were together; we were one. The sweetest spirit filled the room.

During the closing song I heard my "mind" say, "Get up and tell them what it was." I thought, "No, this is the closing song. Thank goodness." Again, my "mind" said, "Get up, and tell them what it was." This time I argued, "No! Here comes the sister to give the closing prayer." Then, a third time, a very firm but very still and small voice came again, "Get up now!"

I scared the poor woman when I jumped up just as she

stepped up to the pulpit to pray. "Excuse me," I said. "Do you know that feeling we all felt these last twenty minutes? Well, that is the Holy Ghost."

That was all. I sat down and never thought another thought about it until a year later when a letter arrived from a woman who had been in attendance that night. She wrote:

"I had been inactive for two years. I had asked my bishop to please excommunicate me. My friend asked me to please attend one last meeting before I went through with this severe step. It seemed harmless enough, and she had been a great support.

"The reason I sought excommunication was that, growing up in the Church, I had heard most of the members speak of the Holy Ghost as someone real to them. He was not real to me. I believed if I had never felt the Spirit I could not know the Church was true and should not be a member.

"When you stood up and said what you did about the Holy Ghost, my heart pounded! I had felt the change in the room the last part of the meeting. When you said it was the Holy Ghost, I knew it was! But something else important, I realized I had felt that same feeling *many* times all my life and just didn't know what it was!"

Books have been written by qualified people, especially General Authorities, on recognizing the Holy Ghost and his mission and purpose. These pages aren't intended to add to such great words from such great men and women. Instead, this book is my witness that everyone starts at the beginning in spiritual scholarship, and we all learn "line upon line, precept upon precept; here a little, and there a little."

A stake president related how he had remained faithful and hopeful over the years through all sorts of problems in life. He said one day he sat interviewing a couple who were in deep despair, their faith wavering. Completely hopeless, they had quit coming to church. He suddenly realized the problem they were struggling with was identical to one he and his wife had had many years before. Then he began to realize that many of the problems he heard across his desk as a bishop and stake president were not unlike his own in life. He wondered why he had been able to remain full of faith and hope when others had given up.

He concluded by saying that also in his life have been many great moments with the Holy Ghost. During the dark hours of trial he would ponder the memories of past spiritual experiences. He said that whenever he felt the hopelessness of whatever trial he was experiencing, he would dwell on past victories and the times he had felt the Spirit strongly. He would pause and bear his testimony to himself and seek the Spirit again as he immersed himself in the scriptures.

We cannot ever forget in the dark hours what the Lord has shown us in the light by the power of the Holy Ghost, our Comforter.

There is a difference between sorrow and suffering. We can be sorrowful and yet "be of good cheer." Being of good cheer is really another way to say we are full of hope. The sorrow never left during Jason's five years of drug abuse, but the suffering did.

We have to *choose* to be of good cheer. We can do that because we are "free to act and not be acted upon." The first time I tried to choose to be of good cheer was hard. I had been used to murmuring and whimpering when things went wrong. But that was years ago. The sale of our house had fallen through only a few days before we were to close. We were packed and ready to go. We had been eating off paper plates for two weeks. My first impulse was to whine, "Oh no, what are we going to do?"

This time I decided to *choose* differently. I decided to

choose to be of good cheer. It wasn't easy. The worry was still there — it never really left until the problem was solved. But I was free to choose, to make a conscious choice to be of good cheer, and I spent a lot of time battling negative thoughts. When they crept forward, I had to choose again, and again, and again. But I discovered it was possible to smile at others, even to avoid complaining, and when asked how it "was going," to respond with "great." At first it was like pretending. But it soon turned into something else. It was a *power* I felt. I could do *something*, I could control the dark thoughts.

As the years have gone by I've practiced being of good cheer. There was plenty of opportunity during Jason's trials. But slowly and surely it became easier and easier to be of good cheer. The more we do something, the more expert we become at doing it. I recall one afternoon when I received a negative phone call and some bad news about business. It hadn't been a good week anyway. I went upstairs and lay down on my bed, crushed, weighed down by the news. Then the thought came to me, "In an hour you are going to have to get up and fix dinner and get on with the evening's activities. Why not get up now, be of good cheer, and save yourself a wasted hour?"

We always seem to end up having to depend on good cheer anyway. Why don't we *choose* to have it at the beginning of our trials and save ourselves "wasted hours"?

If the Savior were here today and you went to see him, would you do what he asked of you? If your burdens were laid at his feet and you felt his Spirit, would you take his advice?

It seems to me that in his presence we would do whatever he asked. When we read his scriptures with the Spirit, his presence is real. The advice in the scriptures is what he would give if he were present. "Lift up your head and be of good cheer" (3 Nephi 1:13). He counsels, "Be of good cheer, and do not fear, for I the Lord am with you, and will stand by you"

(D&C 68:6). The advice is from him, personally, with a promise of his presence. Will we choose to do it, or not?

Enduring to the end with good cheer requires stretching for more patience. Feasting, and not snacking, on the scriptures helps stretch out that patience. It gives us time to ponder, to think, to weigh the experiences we are having with the principles of the gospel.

Patience is such a great virtue of strength. A patient person can be counted on in times of great stress. How patient God must be with all of us as we struggle to overcome "the natural man." How patient and long-suffering he is to let us figure things out and learn to choose wisely through our own experiences.

As Jason struggled with his addictions, I was struggling for patience. Eventually I prayed that the Lord would, in his own due time, bless Jason with the things he needed for change of heart. *"In the Lord's own due time"* is a hard one for most of us. We say we came here for a trial of our faith, but when those trials come, we want witnesses before or during those experiences, even though we know in our hearts we "receive no witness until after the trial of [our] faith" (Ether 12:6).

Right after learning that Jason had been stabbed and had almost died, I was so overwhelmed that I nearly called a friend to send me two huge wrestlers he knew. Why couldn't we send them to tie Jason up and dry him out? If he could only be cleaned up, maybe he could see how bad off he was.

Steve's words of counsel were also of comfort, cooling a mother's heart that burned with grief. Gently he said, "No, Anita. We *can't* do that. He is in the Lord's hands. We put him there, remember? We turned him back to the Savior years ago. Are you trying to tell the Lord he doesn't know his work? We could even be detrimental to Jason's repentance, if we try to force things before he is ready. We must be patient. The Lord knows when the time is right. And he will let us know our part and when we should act."

I went back to mountain-climbing school.

When President Benson was an apostle he said:

"There are times when you simply have to righteously hang on and outlast the devil until his depressive spirit leaves you. While you are going through your trial, you can recall your past victories and count the blessings that you do have with a sure *hope* of greater ones to follow if you are faithful" (*Ensign*, Nov. 1974, pp. 65–67).

The night Jason left was traumatic for the whole family. The other children were sobbing and hanging on his clothing, begging him please, please, not to leave. I could not bear to ride the forty-five minutes each way to the airport, and the other children needed me to stay with them and comfort them. Besides, Steve always said the right thing. Perhaps he could be inspired to say the right words that would soften Jason's heart and he would come back. I even prayed for that the whole time they were gone.

Steve returned about two hours later. I almost expected to see Jason with him. Of course he wasn't. Steve then told me of how they had driven to the airport, bought the tickets, and gone to the gate—all in silence. Then he put his arms around Jason and immediately he felt the power of the Holy Ghost. He told me that he knew what he told Jason next was complete inspiration. He said, "Son, if I never get to raise you again, I want you to go on a mission."

My heart sank. Why did he say that? This isn't what I wanted him to say. This isn't going to bring him back. As the years passed we spoke of that from time to time. During the dark days we thought about that moment of truth and light. Our *hope* was that it was information Jason needed to hear and the Lord would use it. It enabled us to pray during those years not just for his freedom from drugs but also for his choosing to go on a mission. We thought perhaps Steve's words had been said mostly so we would remain hopeful.

About a week after Jason returned from the wilderness experience, he said, "Mom, I want to tell you one of the main reasons I'm going on a mission." Then he shared his memory of that night at the airport five years earlier. He said, "I never forgot those words. They kept coming back to me. I thought about them even at times when I shouldn't have because of what I was doing."

We have added this experience to our reserves to think about it as the trials yet to come bear down upon us and we "simply have to righteously hang on."

We are going to have sorrow in this life. We came here to experience the fullness of mortal life and "an opposition in all things" (2 Nephi 2:11) so that we might truly know joy. Jason was once my greatest sorrow; now he is my greatest joy:

"Now no chastening for the present seemeth to be joyous, but grievous: nevertheless afterward it yieldeth the peaceable fruit of righteousness unto them which are exercised thereby. Wherefore lift up the hands which hang down, and the feeble knees; And make straight paths for your feet, lest that which is lame be turned out of the way; but let it rather be healed" (Hebrews 12:11–13).

If a lame leg kept you from running toward the gates of heaven, wouldn't you rather cut it off than lose eternal life? We need to *bear* those burdens with a spirit of good cheer and let the Savior heal our tendency to "de-press."

We are going to have sorrow in this life, and we need to learn how to suffer. We have to suffer so we can better understand the Atonement. One reason for suffering is to find out we don't have to suffer. The Savior already suffered for us in Gethsemane.

Can we really appreciate his victory over the grave? Can we even begin to understand his love for us, so great a love that he would bear so much and suffer so greatly? In those hours as the Atonement began to unfold, even he had not fully comprehended how extreme and excruciating it would be. He went into the garden at Gethsemane "and began to be *sore amazed,* and to be very heavy" (Mark 14:33). Into these moments came all the sorrows of all the human hearts. Somehow he began to suffer the sorrows of us all, spiritual, physical, and emotional.

"And he shall go forth, *suffering pains* and *afflictions* and *temptations* of every kind; and this that the word might be fulfilled which saith he will take upon him the *pains and the sicknesses* of his people.

"And he will take upon him death, that he may loose the bands of death which bind his people; and he will take upon him their infirmities, that his bowels may be filled with mercy, according to the flesh, that he may know according to the flesh how to succor his people according to their infirmities" (Alma 7:11–12; italics added).

"And he cometh into the world that he may save all men if they will hearken unto his voice; for behold, he suffereth the pains of all men, yea, the pains of every living creature, both men, women, and children, who belong to the family of Adam" (2 Nephi 9:21).

"Which suffering caused myself, even God, the greatest of all, to tremble because of pain, and to bleed at every pore, and to suffer both body and spirit—and would that I might not drink the bitter cup, and shrink" (D&C 19:18).

In suffering we learn we don't have to suffer. Only in our extremities do we discover what the scripture means "with his stripes we are healed" (Mosiah 14:5). When our suffering becomes intense enough, if we have enough humility, we learn that it is possible to lay all of our sorrow and heartache on the altar of God and "give it back" to him. "Surely he has borne our griefs, and *carried* our sorrows" (Mosiah 14:4; italics added). As we lay those things back on the altar in faith and hope, we are able to walk away at peace, resolved to be of good cheer. We learn we don't have to suffer, because he already suffered for us in Gethsemane. If he carried us then, he can carry us now. It doesn't mean we won't have sorrow or that we won't still feel the sorrow, but it does mean our suffering will cease.

There is another reason for suffering. One event in Gethsemane seems curious, not completely clear. Why did the Savior want Peter, James, and John to remain awake?

"And he taketh with him Peter and James and John, and began to be sore amazed, and to be very heavy; And saith unto them, My soul is exceeding sorrowful unto death: tarry ye here, and watch.

"And he went forward a little, and fell on the ground, and prayed that, if it were possible, the hour might pass from him. And he said, Abba, Father, all things are possible unto thee; take away this cup from me: nevertheless not what I will, but what thou wilt.

"And he cometh, and findeth them sleeping, and saith unto Peter, Simon, sleepest thou? couldest not thou watch one hour?

"Watch ye and pray, lest ye enter into temptation. The spirit truly is ready, but the flesh is weak.

"And again he went away, and prayed, and spake the same words. And when he returned, he found them asleep again, (for their eyes were heavy,) neither wist they what to answer him" (Matk 14:33–40).

The Savior's suffering was total and complete. He suffered spiritually the sufferings that come from sin. The anguish, guilt, remorse, and sorrows that accompany disobedience and wickedness were borne by him in the agonizing hour. But that was not all.

Somehow all of our sickness, disease, tragedy, despair, fear, and heartbreak were a part of that awful agony. He was sick, physically sick. He had the pain and physical torment of cancer, migraines, worms, influenza, polio, AIDS, and whatever diseases man can have. And there was more. He felt the grief and heartache of our tragedies. He felt our fears and despair. He bled from every pore because he was physically sick and emotionally heartbroken and spiritually stretched, even beyond his own planning and comprehension. He "grew sore amazed," the scripture informs us.

That picture painted of him serenely kneeling by the tree, praying, could not have been what it was really like at all. If he were in that much agony and bleeding from every pore, he needed help. He needed Peter, James, and John to hold on to him, to steady his tormented, writhing body, to offer words of encouragement and comfort. A passage in Psalms refers to that moment:

"Reproach hath broken my heart; and I am full of heaviness: and I looked for some to take pity, but there was none; and *for comforters, but I found none*" (Psalm 69:20; italics added).

No wonder an angel came and administered to him. He might not have made it without that strengthening.

I do not mean to minimize the hours of being nailed to the cross, but as I came to appreciate what happened in Gethsemane, it seems to me the Atonement really took place there.

Gethsemane in Hebrew means "olive press." It is the word for the press used to squeeze the oil from the olives. How significant! "Ye must *press* forward, with a steadfastness in Christ."

Gethsemane — when that part was over, he knew he could make it. He could go through the rest of it. He could, he could truly, literally, *really* save us. That must have been a great feeling for him. It was his victory!

We struggle to understand just what the Atonement really means to us individually and just how great our Savior is. But there will come a day when we will *know*. At the moment we see him and feel that unbelievable, melting love, we will be aware of all that he suffered for us and know just how much he loves us and just how individual that love is. At that moment, if it hasn't cost us something *personally* to be there, we won't feel worthy of his presence or his gifts to us or of his great, great love. We have to be victorious here so we can be there with glad hearts.

The Savior also had hope. He has a hope in us. The ultimate sacrifice was given because he believes and hopes — expects — many will follow him. So did the writers of the Old and New Testaments; so did the authors of the Book of Mormon. Otherwise without that hope they were painstakingly keeping records and being martyred for nothing. Joseph and Hyrum Smith believed many would follow; they gave their lives as a witness of that hope. We too must believe we can lay hold of eternal life.

While attending Brigham Young University, I heard Elder Hugh B. Brown deliver a devotional address to an assembly gathered in the Smith Fieldhouse. Not much of what he said stayed with me, except his closing remarks. They were almost unbelievable to me.

He was failing in health. He was so feeble he had to be escorted to the podium by President Wilkinson and the student body president. Someone remained at his side while he delivered his address. His closing words were, "I pray *constantly* that I will endure to the end."

It was almost unbelievable. Here was an elderly, feeble, apostle of the Lord saying he hoped he could endure to the end. I immediately thought, "He doesn't really mean that! How could he? He has it made — after all, he is an apostle. But on top of that what could he possibly worry about? His body is too feeble."

My understanding of what he meant has come in full force as life has unfolded and there have been mountains of doubt to climb.

"Endure to the end." Remember how Ammon felt when he and his brothers had completed their mission to the Lamanites? (see Alma 26:11–12). He was full of love and joy and hope. He bore a beautiful testimony of self-esteem. He said his heart was "brim with joy" because they had been obedient and gone on their missions. As to his own strength, he was weak and had nothing to boast for himself, but he would "boast of my God, for in his strength I can do all things." That is self-esteem! That is hope!

At best we are only a short time away from losing self-esteem. We must *try* to be consistent in striving to be obedient. I miss all the time, but I keep trying. If I stop trying, stop reading the scriptures, stop going to church, stop saying prayers, stop going to the temple, stop doing Church work and service, then I might wake up a few weeks from now, empty, full of darkness, depression, and hopelessness.

We have got to keep on trying. Every once in a while we need to rest, ponder, and reflect on our progress, as insignificant as it seems to be. We don't often see the growth in ourselves, but we are growing if we are striving and trying.

My eighteen-year-old daughter was irritated with me about something I had done. She said, "Mother, you just didn't handle that well at all! I would have done it a lot better and much differently!" There was once a day I would have responded curtly with something like, "Really? Well, you need to mature a little more to understand my actions. After all, you are *only* eighteen."

But my response that day was much different. I said, "I hope so! I hope you do everything better than I do. I want you to exceed me and become much more than what I am. That's why I am alive and working so hard at life and motherhood, Ashley. I want my children to take what they have learned from me and go out and be better, do better, rise higher!"

That eternal perspective is for me a brightness of hope. It may be a little light, but it is at least some light.

The darkness and discouragement of the evil one are ever present. It is the "press against" us. His words and influence cripple us, make us doubt ourselves. The least degree of his efforts is enough to knock the spiritual wind out of us. Even while I was preparing this material, an overwhelmingly depressive spirit hung over me one day. Thoughts bombarded me and suddenly, there it was again, that mountain of doubt. "This is a big mistake. No one wants to hear about personal things and experiences. You are making a big mistake." Later, when seeking the comfort of the Spirit and reassurance, one sentence came to mind: "What do you think the scriptures are about?"

Instantly I remembered Nephi's opening words, the story of his family problems, his mountain of doubt, the hope he learned personally. Then all the stories of the repentance and struggles of so many and their individual witnesses and testimonies flooded my thoughts. That one sentence restored "a perfect brightness of hope." I pictured you reading this, and your sorrows became real, if only for a moment. I pictured you feeling a chance to hope again, and for another brief moment, my love for you was personal and one to one.

Some are going to have to struggle all of their lives to overcome sorrow or sin. Some whose burdens of personal weakness are indeed enormous have shared with me their feelings of discouragement and frustration. Not one of us is free from the aching muscles we endure under the weight of personal burdens.

But some are more heavily weighed down as effort to change becomes a daily vigil and a constant watch in obedience. That is what enduring to the end is. Take heart — hope is brightened because discouragement and frustration would not be present in the heart of an unbeliever. What a good feeling it is to know you have the desire to *do* the right thing!

Be of good cheer, fellow Saint. Can't you feel the Savior's love reaching across the eternities to hold us close and guide us safely home? His hand is everywhere. Don't let go of it. Hold on tightly and endure to the end. You can make it. It won't be the same if we aren't all there.

Consider the words of Moroni. He was all alone. His father was dead, and so were his family and friends. Soon he too would be gone. He had witnessed the destruction of his nation, his people. He had seen us in our generation (Mormon 8:35). He had been shown our pride and strife, wars and destructions. He was about to bury the records he had so carefully protected, to come forth in a future world. What would he write as his final words to readers not yet born? What closing lines should he engrave that would carry the message of his heart, his life, his hope?

"I would exhort you that ye would *come unto Christ,* and lay hold upon every good gift, and touch not the evil gift, nor the unclean thing . . . strengthen thy stakes and enlarge thy borders forever, that thou mayest no more be confounded . . . *come unto Christ,* and be perfected in him, and deny yourselves of all ungodliness; and if ye shall deny yourselves of all ungodliness, and love God with all your might, mind and strength, then is his grace sufficient for you, that by his grace ye may be perfect in Christ" (Moroni 10:30–32; italics added).

"Come unto Christ" was his hope for us. It is the hope of all the prophets. It is the hope of the Savior. If all these believe in us and *hope* we can make it, we must "press forward" and "endure to the end" and never, never give up.

Worldwide peace is gone and will not return until the Savior comes again. Does this mean the world is hopeless and we should give up? No! We continue to pray for peace, we continue to pray for countries to be opened to the missionaries, we continue to pray with hope for the world. Yes, the prophecies of destruction are true, and we are now seeing calamity of every kind on every shore. But never has there been so great an army of missionaries in the field—more than forty thousand at this writing. In the years ahead the earth will be flooded with an even greater number of missionaries with the Book of Mormon. A different kind of peace will yet give hope to millions. And millions of members of the true church of Jesus Christ will never, never give up!

While Jason was in the wilderness program, one of the other children expressed great doubt and worry over this effort to save him. What if it didn't work? We were spending a lot of money. She was greatly disturbed. She didn't want us to be hurt again. She didn't want to be hurt again. She didn't want us to lose our money. What would we do if he came home and went back to drugs?

We simply said, "He might. It's a chance. But, if he does, we will never, *never* give up!"

President David O. McKay once said: "I . . . fell asleep, and beheld in vision something infinitely sublime. In the distance I beheld a beautiful white city. Though far away, yet I seemed to realize that trees with luscious fruit, shrubbery with gorgeously-tinted leaves, and flowers in perfect bloom abounded everywhere. The clear sky above seemed to reflect these beautiful shades of color. I then saw a great concourse of people approaching the city. Each one wore a white flowing robe, and a white headdress. Instantly my attention seemed centered upon their Leader, and though I could see only the profile of his features and his body, I recognized him at once as my Savior! The tint and radiance of his countenance were glorious to behold! There was a peace about him which seemed sublime — it was divine!

"The city, I understood, was his. It was the City Eternal; and the people following him were to abide there in peace and eternal happiness.

"But who were they?

"As if the Savior read my thoughts, he answered by pointing to a semicircle that then appeared above them, and on which were written in gold the words:

" *'These Are They Who Have Overcome The World —*
Who Have Truly Been Born Again!' "

(*Cherished Experiences from the Writings of President David O. McKay*, comp. Clare Middlemiss [Salt Lake City: Deseret Book Co., 1965], p. 102.)

All of us are going to come to the end of our mortal lives. Whether that is in a day from now, in a decade, or in a "twinkling of an eye," we can be assured that time will end and we will once again become part of eternity.

If our vision of that eternity is lighted only by a glimmer of hope, it may be too dim in the dark days ahead to see the Gate. But if our vision of eternity is illuminated by a perfect brightness of hope, there is not a chance in the world we will miss the Entrance to Eternal Life.